Susanne Patig

with the collaboration of Juliana Vanessa Casanova-Brito

BPM Software and Process Modelling Languages in Practice

Susanne Patig
with the collaboration of Juliana Vanessa Casanova-Brito

BPM Software and Process Modelling Languages in Practice

Results from an empirical investigation

Frank & Timme

Verlag für wissenschaftliche Literatur

Even where not specifically stated, all names of hardware, software and other goods as well as brand names and trade names used in the book are the property of the respective companies and are generally subject to protection under trademark, brand name or patent law.

ISBN 978-3-86596-396-3

© Frank & Timme GmbH Verlag für wissenschaftliche Literatur
Berlin 2012. Alle Rechte vorbehalten.

Das Werk einschließlich aller Teile ist urheberrechtlich geschützt. Jede Verwertung außerhalb der engen Grenzen des Urheberrechtsgesetzes ist ohne Zustimmung des Verlags unzulässig und strafbar. Das gilt insbesondere für Vervielfältigungen, Übersetzungen, Mikroverfilmungen und die Einspeicherung und Verarbeitung in elektronischen Systemen.

Herstellung durch das atelier eilenberger, Taucha bei Leipzig.
Printed in Germany.
Gedruckt auf säurefreiem, alterungsbeständigem Papier.

www.frank-timme.de

CONTENTS

CONTENTS 5

LIST OF TABLES AND FIGURES 7

LIST OF SYMBOLS AND ABBREVIATIONS 9

1 Introduction 11

2 Research Background 13

3 Research Method 15
    3.1 Research Goals 15
    3.2 Materials 16
    3.3 Procedure 16
    3.4 Participants 16

4 Results of the World-Wide Survey 19
    4.1 Reporting of the Results 19
    4.2 Characteristics of Business Processes 19
    4.3 Software in Business Process Management 29
    4.4 Describing Business Processes 35

5 Interpretation of the Empirical Results 47
    5.1 Discussion of the Findings 47
    5.2 Current BPM Maturity from the IT Perspective 50
        5.2.1 Measuring BPM Maturity 50
        5.2.2 IT-related BPM Maturity implied by the Survey 54
    5.3 Evaluation of Common Process Modelling Languages 55
        5.3.1 Widespread Process Modelling Languages 55
        5.3.2 Survey-based Assessment of Evaluation Frameworks 60
        5.3.3 Survey-based Comparison of Process Modelling Languages 62

6 Limitations of the Investigation 67

7 Conclusions 69

APPENDIX A: QUESTIONNAIRE 71

APPENDIX B: COVER LETTERS FOR THE QUESTIONNAIRE 79

REFERENCES 83

LIST OF TABLES AND FIGURES

Table 3-1: Numbers of responses per sector and per region - Q39 17
Table 3-2: Affiliation of participants (and organization of process modelling) - Q1** 18
Table 3-3: Process overview of participants – Q2** 18
Table 4-1: Distribution of processes – Q33 20
Table 4-2: Statistics for an average process - Q34 21
Table 4-3: Timing of processes according to modes - Q35, Q36 21
Table 4-4: Process scope per region - Q15 22
Table 4-5: Process scope per department - Q15** 22
Table 4-6: Typical process descriptions per region – Q13 23
Table 4-7: Triggers of processes per region - Q17(**) 24
Table 4-8: Applications involved in process execution per region - Q18 24
Table 4-9: Triggers of processes per department - Q17 25
Table 4-10: Applications involved in process execution per department - Q18** 26
Table 4-11: Frequency of process change per region - Q27 26
Table 4-12: Amount of process change per region - Q28** 27
Table 4-13: Amount of process change per department - Q28 27
Table 4-14: Impact of process change per region - Q29 27
Table 4-15: Impact of process change per department - Q29 27
Table 4-16: Reasons for process change per region - Q30** 28
Table 4-17: Reasons for process change per department – Q30 28
Table 4-18: Coping with process change per region - Q31 28
Table 4-19: Coping with process change per department - Q31 28
Table 4-20: Currently used BPM software per region - Q11** 29
Table 4-21: Currently used BPM software per department - Q11** 30
Table 4-22: Decision criteria for BPM software selection per region - Q12 (**) 30
Table 4-23: Decision criteria for BPM software selection per department - Q12(*) 31
Table 4-24: Important functionalities and qualities for BPM tools per region – Q8 (**) 31
Table 4-25: Important functionalities and qualities for BPM tools per department – Q8 (**) 32
Table 4-26: Required kind of support for process execution per region– Q9 32
Table 4-27: Required kind of support for process execution per department- Q9 34
Table 4-28: Information wished to be monitored per region – Q10 35
Table 4-29: Information wished to be monitored per department – Q10 35
Table 4-30: Reasons to describe processes per region – Q5** 37
Table 4-31: Reasons to describe processes per department – Q5 37
Table 4-32: Process models in non-BPM software per region – Q6 37
Table 4-33: Current documentation of processes per region – Q4 ** 38
Table 4-34: Current documentation of processes per department – Q4** 38
Table 4-35: Company-internal organization of process design – Q3 39
Table 4-36: Procedure for process design per region - Q16 39

Table 4-37: Procedure for process design per department - Q16 39
Table 4-38: Basic concepts in process models per region - Q19 40
Table 4-39: Task relationships per region - Q20 40
Table 4-40: Basic concepts in process models per department - Q19 41
Table 4-41: Task relationships per department - Q20 41
Table 4-42: Execution of succeeding tasks per region - Q21 42
Table 4-43: Execution of succeeding tasks per department - Q21 42
Table 4-44: Nature of conditions per region – Q21A 43
Table 4-45: Nature of conditions per department – Q21A 43
Table 4-46: Required information about persons per region – Q23 44
Table 4-47: Required information about persons per department – Q23 44
Table 4-48: Resources needed in process models per region - Q22(**) 44
Table 4-49: Resources needed in process models per department - Q22(**) 45
Table 4-50: Additional concepts needed in process models - Q24 46
Table 4-51: Additional concepts needed in process models - Q24 (**) 46
Table 5-1: Summary of the findings 49
Table 5-2: Selected BPM maturity models 51
Table 5-3: BPM maturity from the IT perspective in the literature and the questionnaire 53
Table 5-4: BPM maturity from the IT view per region 54
Table 5-5: Main constructs of the most widespread process modelling languages 57
Table 5-6. Considered requirements in prominent evaluation frameworks for process modelling languages 61
Table 5-7. Expressiveness of prominent process modelling languages 63

Figure 4-1: Average business process from a statistical point of view 20
Figure 4-2: Important functionalities and qualities for BPM tools per department – Q8 (**) 33
Figure 4-3: Reasons to describe processes per Region – Q5 36
Figure 4-4: Reasons to describe processes per department – Q5 36
Figure 5-1: Extract of an order management process as BPMN diagram 55
Figure 5-2: Extract of an order management process as UML activity diagram 58
Figure 5-3: Extract of an order management process as extended Event-driven process chain 59

LIST OF SYMBOLS AND ABBREVIATIONS

** / *	Statistically significant results ($\alpha = 0.05$) / ($\alpha = 0.1$)
α	Probability of error
μ	Arithmetic Mean
σ	Standard Deviation
Σ	Sum
χ^2_{ma}	Test statistic of the modified Pearson chi-square test
c_i	Count of answers for an answer option i
c_o	Count of answers for an open question
df	Degrees of freedom
H	Test statistic of the Kruskal-Wallis
N	Number of valid responses for a question (per region or department)
N^+	Total number of participating companies ($N^+ = 130$)
N^+_{NA}	Total number of participating companies from North America ($N^+_{NA} = 26$)
N^+_{EU}	Total number of participating companies from Europe ($N^+_{EU} = 75$)
N^+_O	Total number of participating companies from 'other' countries ($N^+_O = 29$)
na	Missing Value
p	Calculated probability of the test statistics χ^2_{ma} and H, respectively

BPEL	Business Process Execution Language
BPM	Business Process Management
BPMN	Business Process Model and Notation
BWW	Bunge-Wand-Weber representation model
CMM(I)	Capability Maturity Model (Integration)
CO	Department for Company Organization
CRM	Customer Relationship Management
eEPC	Extended Event-driven Process Chain
EIU	Economist Intelligence Unit
EPC	Event-driven Process Chain
ERP	Enterprise Resource Planning
EU	Europe
FA	Functional Area
HR	Human Resource
IDEF	Integrated Definition (language family)
IT	Information Technology
LNCS	Lecture Notes in Computer Science
ML	Maturity Level
NA	North America
O	Other countries (see Section 3.4)
OASIS	Organization for the Advancement of Structured Information Standards
OMG	Object Management Group
P	Property
S	Stereotype
SCM	Supply Chain Management
UML	Unified Modelling Language
WF	Workflow
WFCP	Workflow control pattern
WFDP	Workflow data pattern
WFEH	Workflow exception handling pattern
WfMC	Workflow Management Coalition
XPDL	XML Process Definition Language

1 Introduction

Business process management (BPM) comprises the analysis, design, implementation, enactment, monitoring and improvement of business processes [zuMu04]. *Business processes* are sets of linked *activities* (i.e. tasks to be done) that collectively realize a business objective or policy goal within the context of an organizational structure [WfMC99]. For brevity, we omit the term 'business' in the following and just speak about *processes* wherever appropriate.

The number of companies that adopt BPM to reduce costs or improve productivity and customer satisfaction has been constantly increasing since 2005 [WoHa10]. However, the companies' capabilities in BPM (i.e. their *BPM maturity*) are still rather rudimentary. A distinction is typically drawn between the following *levels of BPM maturity* (for details see Section 5.2.1):

- *Level 1:* (business) processes are not defined or are ad-hoc; the organization is around functional areas, product lines or geographic regions
- *Level 2:* some processes are defined and documented; general software is used
- *Level 3:* all process are defined and documented; BPM is applied with strategic intent; BPM tools (software for modelling and analyzing processes) are used
- *Level 4:* all processes are measured and controlled; processes are automated by BPM systems
- *Level 5*: process automation involves business partners; IT is agile.

Empirical investigations indicate that most companies in the USA and Europe are on BPM maturity Level 2 or between the Levels 2 and 3 [WoHa10]; the higher levels of BPM maturity (Levels 4 and 5) are not yet reached.

It is generally accepted that BPM maturity depends on several success factors such as people, culture, strategic alignment and IT [MeSi06]. *Information technology (IT)* has turned out to be a key factor for reaching the higher levels (4 and 5) of BPM maturity [McWB+09]. Thus the low current BPM maturity of the companies can indicate (1) the companies' insufficient IT capabilities, (2) the software's inability to satisfy BPM-specific requirements, which prevents it from being used in the companies, or (3) difficulties and inconsistencies in assessing BPM maturity (see the arguments in [BeKP09].

The investigation presented in this book mainly addresses the second issue: it aims to find out how companies currently use IT to support BPM and which (possibly unsatisfied) requirements they have in this respect. Though hardware such as RFID transponders, barcode scanners or point-of-sale terminals can also advance processes and are part of IT, their usage is not investigated here. Instead, the focus is on *software for BPM*, which can be classed as general software, BPM tool, BPM system or BPM suite. *General software* comprises *applications* that are not intended for BPM, but support users in performing any kind of task. Examples are text processing systems, simple graphics tools, databases or Enterprise Resource Planning (ERP) systems. In contrast, BPM tools, BPM systems and BPM suites were designed for BPM. *BPM tools* (e.g. iGrafx[1], SemTalk) facilitate process modelling and often also the analysis of process models (e.g. by simulation), but they do not support process automation, which is the task of *BPM systems* (e.g. IBM Websphere). Finally, *BPM suites* (e.g. Oracle BPM, TIBCO iProcess Suite) combine features from BPM tools and BPM systems. In practice, the boundaries between the three types of BPM software become blurred.

The investigation presented here covers the use of software during the whole life cycle of BPM from process analysis to improvement. It was conducted from June to December 2009 among companies from the 'Forbes Global 2000' list. Parts of the results have been published before at various conferences [PaCV10], [PaCa11]. This book contains all data as well as additional descriptive statistics. It was written to support scientists in identifying interesting research questions; to show vendors of BPM tools, systems and suites which improvements of their software are necessary, and to give companies a rule of thumb estimate of their organization's BPM capabilities.

After summarizing existing empirical investigations in the field of BPM in Chapter 2, we describe our research method in Chapter 3. Chapter 4 contains the results concerning processes, software for BPM and process modelling. In Chapter 5 the results are used to assess both the current BPM maturity of several regions of the world from the IT perspective and the most widespread process modelling languages. Comments on the limitations of the investigation and the reliability as well as validity of the gathered results can be found in Chapter 6.

---

[1] All names of products and services are trademarks, service marks or registered companies, even if not explicitly stated.

2 Research Background

Several empirical studies in the field of BPM have been published in recent years; these are summarized briefly in this section. The main differences between the studies are their *focus* (management, BPM software, process modelling), the *object* of research (company assessments, experts, BPM software, process models) and the *research method* (cases, surveys, samples of process diagrams and a Delphi study). Studies conducted by vendors of BPM software are excluded here because they are potentially biased.

The oldest empirical study stems from 1999 and explores the importance, understanding and realization of *business process management* in European companies [PrAr99]. Based on a survey and case studies (gathered by interviews with senior executives of the companies), the drivers and the degree of BPM implementation at that time were identified. It turned out that BPM adoption in most companies was impelled by strategic imperatives such as increased customer satisfaction, quality or productivity. As an answer to these imperatives, the companies identified a few business processes and process owners at the highest organizational level. Then, these top-level processes were broken down into detailed processes that finally changed the task level at which teams and individuals operate. At that time, the single greatest difficulty in implementing BPM was the lack of BPM understanding in the companies. Altogether, about 100 business experts were surveyed. The survey only took an organizational view; neither BPM software nor process modelling languages were considered.

A more recent case study, in which seven senior managers of the same large UK bank were interviewed about process strategy, process architecture, process ownership, process measurement and process improvement [SmMM09], yielded similar results, e.g. processes are defined to increase customer satisfaction. BPM software was neglected. Because only a single company was used as a case study, the derived integrated framework for BPM (managerial point of view only) cannot be considered valid.

In 2009, based on assessments of hundreds of companies in the USA, Europe, China and Brazil, the key turning points in *business process maturity* were identified [McWB+09]; process documentation, knowing the customer and endorsing teamwork proved necessary at BPM maturity Level 2. Process measurement and a process language (in the sense of corporation-wide process terms) appeared to be important in order to reach BPM maturity Level 3. Finally, process-oriented jobs and support by BPM software were needed for the transition to BPM maturity Level 4. The BPM maturity assessment used was specific (see Section 5.2.1). Neither specifics of process modelling languages or software were considered.

Some investigations (e.g., [Neub09], [WoHa10]) combine questions on managerial issues of BPM and BPM software – to account for the software's importance for reaching the higher levels of BPM maturity. The study "Status Quo of BPM" [Neub09] asked decision makers of 185 companies from Germany, Austria and Switzerland (mainly IT-driven sectors) about the alignment between BPM and business strategy, and about process management methods, the organization of BPM and the role of IT. It showed that mainly proprietary systems and ERP systems influence the companies' business processes; systems for Supply Chain Management (SCM) have lost importance for BPM. BPM suites were far less important. If companies use a BPM suite, they mostly apply its process modelling and process publication functionalities; the functionalities of process simulation, modelling and controlling were also mentioned. The software was mostly selected in the companies by mixed teams with members from business, IT and organization departments. The poor reporting of the tool-related questions in the paper affects their reliability overall.

The report "State of Business Process Management 2010" [WoHa10] focussed on the understanding of BPM in companies, the BPM drivers, maturity and current activities. 264 companies from all over the world were surveyed. The major BPM drivers mentioned were reducing cost and improving productivity, coordination, organizational responsiveness as well as customer satisfaction. Only three questions dealt with BPM software. They showed that companies mainly rely on simple graphics tools and repository-based modelling tools. Only 26 % of the companies use a BPM system or suite, and only 16 % believe that this is important for BPM. The dominant BPM suite is IBM WebSphere BPM. According to this investigation, most companies seem to be at BPM maturity Level 2 or between the BPM maturity Levels 2 and 3.

Most *tool-related studies* (e.g. [Schm08], [JaBS06]) are lightweight versions of the Gartner Group's 'Magic Quadrants' for BPM suites [SiHi10] and business process analysis tools [NoBJ10], where BPM software is evaluated based on a set of criteria. The actual use of this software in companies is not considered there.

Beside such evaluations, *cases of implementing business processes* with BPM systems have been reported in conjunction with the realized benefits and the encountered challenges [KüHa07]. Over four BPM projects, the use of BPM systems lead to reduced cycle time as well as to increased output per employee and quality of work. The process monitoring enabled by BPM systems was rated especially beneficial because it helped in identifying and improving poor parts of a process. The biggest challenge arose from the fact that general packaged software (commercial off-the-shelf software) is becoming increasingly important for financial institutions, but often does not offer cost-efficient integration mechanisms for BPM systems.

Process modelling is a fundamental step of BPM because it not only documents business processes, but also prepares all future BPM activities. In a language-neutral Delphi study, 62 experts from practice, academia and software vendors were asked about the benefits, issues and challenges of process modelling. Process improvement, understanding and communication emerged as overall (across all three stakeholder groups) benefits of process modelling [InRR09a], whereas standardization, the value proposition of process modelling to business and model-driven process execution are currently seen as main overall issues and challenges [InRR09b].

So far, the requirements for *process modelling languages* have been derived from the process modelling literature (e.g. [LiKo06], [SöAJ+02]), from BPM methods [LiYP02], from ontologies such as the Bunge-Wand-Weber (BWW) representation model (e.g. [GrRo00]) or from workflow patterns (e.g. [RuHA+06]). The resulting evaluation frameworks are discussed in Section 5.3.2. Empirical investigations of the companies' requirements for process modelling languages are sparse and mainly focus on the *Business Process Model and Notation (BPMN)* [OMG11]. The following results deserve closer attention.

The *Bunge-Wand-Weber representation model* is a philosophically founded ontology of what exists in reality and, thus, can be represented in information systems. It was used to derive and test hypotheses about the constructs that are missing, redundant, superfluous and overloaded in the BPMN [ReIR+06]. The hypotheses were tested in interviews with nineteen participants from Australian organizations. It turned out that the support provided by the BPMN for state modelling is insufficient and that constructs which do not have a real-world meaning (e.g. looping, multiple instances) are difficult to understand. Lack of understandability also holds true for the constructs 'pool' and 'lane' because they map ambiguously onto entities from the BWW representation model. Additionally, some constructs that are rated as being excessive based on the BWW representation model (e.g. normal flow, event as a supertype, data object, activity looping) are considered essential by 40-50 % of the participants. However, the investigation is biased insofar as all tested hypotheses were only derived from the BWW representation model – and not from the companies' requirements.

Indirectly, the companies' requirements were addressed by an investigation in which a sample of 120 BPMN process models was analyzed to find out which BPMN constructs were used most often [zMRI07], [zMRI08]. The results show that only nine out of the fifty modelling constructs offered by the BPMN in version 1.0 recur in all process models. These constructs (ordered in decreasing frequency) are the following: task, sequence flow, start/end event, pool, general/parallel gateway, lane and XOR gateway. The BPMN therefore seems to be unnecessarily complex. However, observing the usage of language constructs in process models does not answer the questions as to whether these constructs really meet the companies' requirements – or just serve as makeshifts.

Finally, requirements for BPMN modelling tools were examined in a world-wide empirical survey [Reck08]. Based on the answers of 590 experts from industry and academia, simple graphics tools (especially Microsoft Visio) are clearly preferred for modelling with the BPMN. These tools and the created process models are mainly (51 %) used for business purposes such as process documentation, analysis and improvement, yet the other 49 % of the users pursue more technical purposes such as process simulation and workflow engineering. According to this investigation, the most appreciated functionalities of the BPMN software are an integrated repository for process models, facilities for navigating between process models and additional fields for attributes. The BPMN constructs needed in the companies were not analyzed.

Altogether, none of the empirical investigations that have been conducted so far provides comprehensive and detailed information about the companies' requirements concerning software for BPM during the complete BPM life cycle. (Process modelling and process modelling languages belong to the design phase of BPM; see Section 3.1). Revealing these requirements is the goal of our research.

3 Research Method

3.1 Research Goals

The investigation presented in this book was *exploratory* as we aimed at discovering the companies' requirements concerning software throughout the BPM lifecycle. Roughly condensed, the *BPM life cycle* consists of the following phases [zuMu04]:

- Process-related *analysis*, where goals as well as the organizational and technical environment of the business processes are gathered.

- *Process design*, where the processes are formally described and the resources responsible for process execution are assigned. *Process descriptions* can be created with natural languages, technical specification languages such as the BPEL (Business Process Execution Language [OASIS07]) or graphical process modelling languages, e.g. the Business Process Model and Notation − BPMN [OMG11], activity diagrams of the Unified Modelling Language − UML [OMG10] or the event-driven process chain − EPC [ScTA05]. If IT is used for process execution, then process design also includes the necessary *implementation* activities.

- *Process enactment,* where individual process instances are executed in accordance with the process description. Execution can involve technical devices, human participants or various kinds of software (general software, BPM tools, BPM systems, BPM suites; see Section 1).

- *Process monitoring* accompanies process enactment since the results and intermediate steps of process execution are continuously compared to the process descriptions. In case of deviations, short-term corrective actions are triggered. In the long term, process monitoring prepares process improvement.

- *Process improvement* uses the results of process monitoring to change the structure, flow and resources of the processes in order to increase both efficiency and effectiveness of process enactment.

Though no phase was excluded in this investigation, the focus was on process design, enactment and monitoring. These phases are easier to support using software than are process analysis and improvement, which depend on managerial experience and human creativity. Process analysis is considered here primarily from the point of view of results because we assume that these results influence the IT requirements of BPM.

In detail, the investigation presented in this book pursued the following goals:

- *Goal 1*: Exploration of the current usage of software throughout the BPM life cycle
  to conclude from the results on the world-wide BPM maturity − insofar as it is dependent on IT

- *Goal 2*: Identification of the companies' requirements concerning software for BPM
  to guide future development of BPM tools, systems and suites

- *Goal 3*: Identification of the companies' requirements concerning process modelling languages
  to enable a reality-driven assessment of process modelling languages and to guide future language design

These *goals* are *related* since the actual usage of software (Goal 1) already indicates certain requirements. However, to exclude the possibility that a particular software is just being used as a compromise, we also inquired verbatim after IT requirements of distinct BPM activities (Goal 2). Finally, since process modelling is a prerequisite for the use of BPM systems, the requirements gathered by Goal 3 have relevance to software (Goal 2), too.

Altogether we adopted a bird's eye view on the *common* requirements concerning software and process modelling languages, which ignores details about the individual companies and instead emphasizes potential differences between regions and departments. In this way we hoped to obtain a general, realistic, world-wide impression of the state of IT support for BPM and the related requirements.

3.2 Materials

The questionnaire, which can be found in Appendix A, was designed according to the (condensed) phases of the BPM lifecycle, i.e. process analysis, design, enactment, monitoring and improvement. We inquired after the nature of the companies' processes, the various degrees of software involvement in the BPM lifecycle phases, process documentation and socio-demographic information. All questions were partially open-ended, i.e. they provided a list with alternatives and an alternative 'other' for entering free text (unanticipated answers). The answer alternatives were derived from BPM textbooks (e.g. [zuMu04]; [BeKR03]; [vAvH04]; [Holt09]; [Wesk07]; [Chan06]) and other empirical investigations (e.g. [Neub09]; [Reck08]). The most important issues were covered by several questions in order to increase the reliability of the results.

The questionnaire consisted of 42 questions in total. Some questions were optional. The data was collected on *nominal* scales (participants were asked to select *all* alternatives that applied to their case) or on an *ordinal* scale (participants were asked to rate some alternatives or to apply a ranking). All *rating scales* had four levels (to avoid neutral answers) and an additional level (e.g. 'Don't know', 'Not applicable', 'Not needed', 'None') to avoid forced ratings [Jack09]. The resulting total number of five rating levels is generally reckoned to be optimal since the ability to differentiate between ratings decreases with an increasing number of rating levels [Jack09]. In detail, the following *rating scale types* were used:

- *Scale 1*: 1 = Essential, 2 = Frequently needed, 3 = Occasionally needed, 4 = Rarely needed, 5 = Not at all needed
- *Scale 2*: 1 = Always, 2 = Very Often, 3 = Sometimes, 4 = Rarely, 5 = Never
- *Scale 3*: 1 = All processes, 2 = Most processes, 3 = Some processes, 4 = A few processes, 5 = No processes
- *Scale 4*: 1 = Very important, 2 = Important, 3 = Not so important, 4 = Not at all important, 5 = Don't know

The questionnaire, including definitions of key terms used in the questions, was written in English and implemented as an online form with the 'LimeSurvey' tool [Lime09].

3.3 Procedure

We conducted a pretest of the questionnaire with ten BPM experts from practice and academia to check the questions for understandability and unambiguity of responses; afterwards, the questionnaire was revised. Appendix A contains the final questionnaire.

In order to contact the companies, we sent letters by surface mail containing the link to the online form and explaining the goals and importance of our investigation. These letters were written in English, German, Spanish and Japanese – depending on the location of the company's headquarters – to make the goals and importance of our research understandable for the addressees. The letters can be found in Appendix B.

Since little is known about the internal organization of BPM in a company, we sent the letters with the link to the final questionnaire to the CIOs or CEOs of the companies and asked them to forward the letters to the persons responsible for BPM. After four to six weeks, we phoned the offices of the CIOs or CEOs to inquire after the status of our information request. After six to eight weeks, we sent reminder letters by surface mail. The survey was conducted from June to December 2009. No incentives were given; the companies were only offered the opportunity to obtain the results of the investigation free of charge.

3.4 Participants

The basic population for this investigation consisted of the companies from the 'Forbes Global 2000' list [Forb00]. This list is an annual ranking of the top 2,000 public companies in the world based on sales, profit, assets and market value. According to the investigation's focus on software, the requirement was for *e-readiness*, which describes the ability of a country and its businesses to use IT to their benefit [EIU08]. The 'e-readiness' of seventy countries is assessed yearly on a scale from one (lowest) to ten [EIU08]. Since our investigation was conducted in 2009, the e-readiness rating of the year 2008 was used. In this year, the average e-readiness score amounted to 6.4. All companies that are headquartered in countries with below-average e-readiness were discounted. From the remaining list, a sample of 1,172 companies was drawn by random numbers. These were contacted as described in Section 3.3.

In total, $N^+ = 130$ companies responded; the response rate was therefore 11 %. Table 3-1 shows the sector and the geographic region of the participants. The geographic region was determined by the companies' headquarters. *North America (NA)* comprises the USA and Canada; *Europe (EU)* includes companies from Austria, Belgium, Denmark, France, Germany, Greece, Iceland, Ireland, Italy, Luxembourg, the Netherlands, Norway, Portugal, Spain, Sweden, Switzerland and the UK; *other countries (O)* are Australia, Hong Kong, Japan, New Zealand, Singapore and Taiwan. The abbreviations 'NA', 'EU' and 'O' are used in all tables of this book.

Table 3-1: Numbers of responses per sector and per region ($N_{NA} = 26$; $N_{EU} = 75$; $N_O = 29$) - Q39

Sector	Responses per region			Sector	Responses per region		
	NA	EU	O		NA	EU	O
Banking	4	20	6	Drugs & biotechnology	1	2	0
Conglomerates	0	1	0	Semiconductors	1	2	1
Oil & gas operations	2	5	1	Chemicals	2	2	1
Consumer durables	2	0	2	Transportation	1	4	4
Insurance	2	7	0	Trading companies	1	0	2
Diversified financials	2	5	0	Health care equip. & services	0	0	1
Telecommunications service	1	3	1	Aerospace & defence	1	1	2
Retailing	3	2	1	Media	1	2	0
Utilities	0	8	2	Construction	0	4	2
Household & personal products	0	2	1	Capital goods	0	2	2
Materials	3	1	3	Hotels, restaurants & leisure	1	2	0
Software & services	0	2	3	Business services & supplies	0	1	0
Food, drink & tobacco	1	2	1				
Techn. hardware & equip.	3	1	4	**Total**	32	81	40

Companies whose headquarters are located in Europe account for the majority of responses ($N^+_{EU} = 75$; 58 %), followed by 'other' countries ($N^+_O = 29$; 22 %) and North America ($N^+_{NA} = 26$; 20 %). Since some of the companies operate in more than one sector, the sum of the counts in Table 3-1 exceeds the numbers of participants N^+_{EU}, N^+_{NA} and N^+_O.

All sectors are represented. Most responses came from the banking sector (see Section 6 where the limitations of the investigation are discussed), followed by utilities, transportation and insurance, as well as oil & gas and technology hardware.

Most of the companies' representatives who answered the questionnaire work in IT departments, followed by departments for BPM (see Table 3-2). In companies from North America and the 'other' countries, functional areas rank third (or second, respectively), as opposed to European companies where departments for company organization take the third rank. Some representatives work for more than one department, therefore the sum of counts in Table 3-2 is larger than the total number of participants ($N^+ = 130$).

Because of the procedure in which we asked the CIOs or CEOs to forward our letters to the persons responsible for BPM, the answers to Question (Q1) are also indicators of the *organization of BPM* in the companies. Thus the responsibility for BPM seems to be mainly delegated to IT departments. This is especially the case if no distinct department for BPM exists. Departments for BPM are mainly common in European companies. The regional differences are significant ($\chi^2_{ma} = 22.96$; df = 10; p = 0.011), though the validity of the test is possibly affected by the low and unbalanced cell counts (see Section 4.1 for the modified Pearson chi-square test).

Table 3-2: Affiliation of participants (and organization of process modelling) ($N_{NA} = 26$; $N_{EU} = 75$; $N_O = 29$) - Q1**

Answers	Count (c_i)			Percentage ($c_i / \Sigma c_i$)		
	NA	EU	O	NA	EU	O
IT	19	44	25	59.4 %	44.9 %	69.4 %
Business process management (BPM)	5	29	4	15.6 %	29.6 %	11.1 %
Functional area (FA)	5	7	4	15.6 %	7.1 %	11.1 %
Company organization (O)	2	17	3	6.3 %	17.3 %	8.3 %
Product division	1	1	0	3.1 %	1.0 %	0.0 %
Total	32	98	36	100.0 %	100.0 %	100.0 %

The abbreviations for the departments given in Table 3-2 are used in all corresponding tables of this book. Because of the low counts, the department 'product division' is discounted.

In addition to knowledge about the processes of their own departments, most participants from North American and European companies stated that they had a company-wide picture of the processes; see Table 3-3. Representatives of companies from the 'other' countries mostly knew the processes of other departments in addition to their own department. The regional differences are significant for $\alpha = 0.05$ ($\chi^2_{ma} = 14.90$; df = 6; p = 0.021).

Almost half of the participants selected more than one answer option; for this reason the sum of the counts in Table 3-3 is larger than the total number of participants ($N^+ = 130$). Altogether, the participants of our survey had quite a broad overview of the processes in their companies.

Table 3-3: Process overview of participants ($N_{NA} = 26$; $N_{EU} = 75$; $N_O = 29$) – Q2**

Answers	Count (c_i)			Percentage ($c_i / \Sigma c_i$)		
	NA	EU	O	NA	EU	O
Have company-wide picture of processes	18	54	12	48.6 %	52.9 %	29.3 %
Processes of my own department	11	26	16	29.7 %	25.5 %	39.0 %
Processes of other departments	8	22	13	21.6 %	21.6 %	31.7 %
Total	37	102	41	100.0 %	100.0 %	100.0 %

4 Results of the World-Wide Survey

4.1 Reporting of the Results

In the following, we refer to the questions by their number (Q##), which we give in the text and in the headings of the tables. The numbers '##', ranging from 1 to 39, are the same as in the questionnaire, which can be found in Appendix A; it contains the wording of the questions. Some questions were not answered by all companies. Because of the resulting *missing values (na)*, the number of *valid responses N* from a region can be smaller than the *total number of participating companies* from that region (i.e. $N^+_{EU} \leq 75$, $N^+_O \leq 29$ and $N^+_{NA} \leq 26$).

For the questions on *nominal scale* we give the *counts* c_i for each alternative answer. With the exception of question (Q12) we allowed multiple answers ('choose *all* alternatives that apply ...'). As a result, the sum of counts (Σc_i) for an alternative (answer) can exceed the number N of responding companies. The answer alternative with the highest count (absolute frequency) represents the *mode* [GrWa09]. In addition to the count c_i we also give the corresponding *percentage* ($c_i / \Sigma c_i$) for each answer alternative per region or per department. The highest percentages are shaded in the tables. If questions involved entering free text (*open questions*), we just give the *answers* c_o obtained, usually as generalized and condensed wording.

Questions on *ordinal scale* can be recognized by the rating scale type from Section 3.2. According to this rating scale type, a numerical value is associated with each rating level to calculate the *mean rating* (μ) and the *standard deviation* (σ) of ratings; the numerical values 1 and 5 correspond to the highest and the lowest rating, respectively. The highest mean ratings are shaded in the tables.

Basically we assume two kinds of influences on the answers given: the *region* (North America, Europe, 'other' countries) and, especially for the questions discussed in Section 4.3 and Section 4.4, the *department* (IT, BPM, functional area, company organization), in which the participant works. The significance of differences between regions and departments was tested with a *modified Pearson chi-square test* (test statistic χ^2_{ma}) that allows multiple answers [BiLN00], while the *Kruskal-Wallis test* ([Krus52]; test statistic H) was used to test differences in the ratings. Both tests are non-parametric, i.e. they rely on fewer assumptions and are applicable even though the underlying distributions are not known. The modified Pearson chi-square test expects that the cell counts are all larger than one and that more than 80 % of cells have expected cell counts larger than five [BiLN00]. The *null hypothesis* for either test claims equality between the regions and departments, and it can be rejected when the calculated *probabilities p* of the test statistics χ^2_{ma} or H are smaller than the probability of error, which was set to $\alpha = 0.05$. As there is neither theoretical nor empirical evidence of the superiority of any region or department, two-sided alternative hypotheses were used. The test statistics, their probabilities p and the degrees of freedom *df* were calculated with the SPSS software, Version 18 [SPSS10]. For the Pearson chi-square test we added a category 'multiple' to represent participants that work in several departments. Tables that contain significant results are marked by adding '**' for $\alpha = 0.05$ (or '*' for $\alpha = 0.1$) to the number of the question.

In the tables that are relevant to BPM maturity, a column 'ML' for maturity levels exists. It gives the *mean maturity levels* that the answer alternatives indicate. The assessment of BPM maturity is explained in Section 5.2.1.

4.2 Characteristics of Business Processes

Process statistics (Q34): Figure 4-1 shows the average business process from a statistical point of view as it was revealed by our investigation. According to the answers of the companies' representatives, a business process on average consists of nineteen activities that involve four departments, seven persons per department and relies on four (software) applications. Moreover, on average one to two ($\mu = 1.8$) other companies take part in a business process.

These mean values have been calculated from the original, detailed data obtained for Question (Q34). In Table 4-2 we summarize this data by giving the minimum and maximum values as well as the arithmetic means and standard deviations per region. It shows that the average number of involved software applications is the same for all regions. Business processes of North American companies seem to consist of more activities,

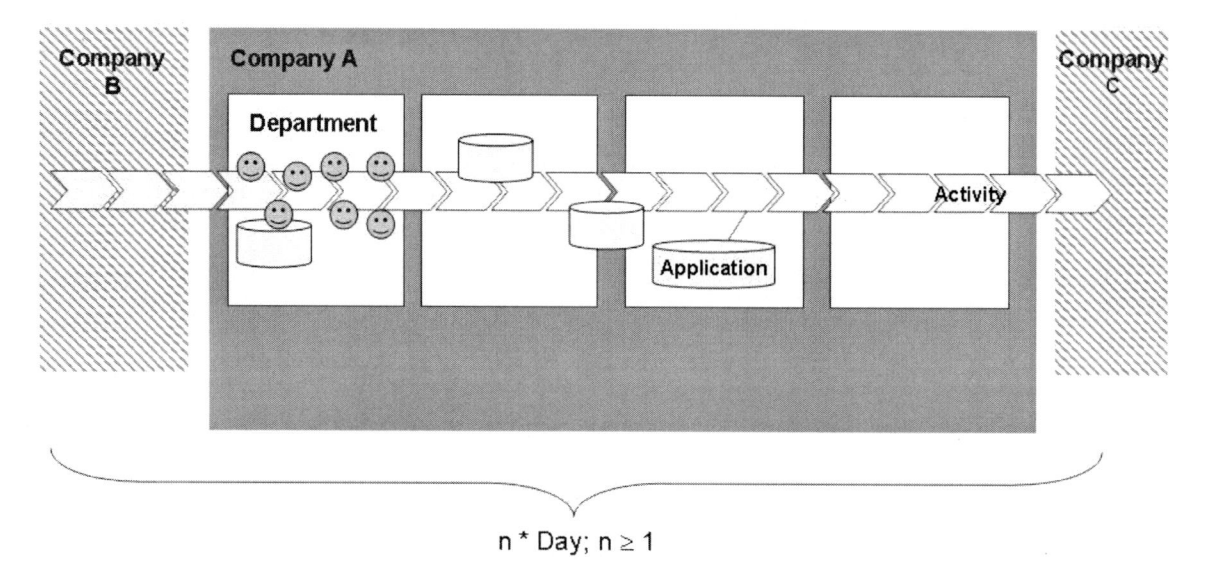

Figure 4-1: Average business process from a statistical point of view

involve more persons per department and more companies. However, since the regional mean values were calculated from the participants' estimates, they should not be taken literally.

Process distribution (Q33) was analyzed by a complementary, more qualitative question. The columns of Table 4-1 correspond to the rating scale of Type 3 (see Section 3.2), where the extreme ratings 'all processes' and 'no process' were omitted because of the sparse responses. The rows of Table 4-1 reflect the answer alternatives of the survey, and the cells show the most frequent rating (i.e. the mode) for each alternative. Most processes in North America and Europe remain within the companies and span several departments. Especially in the 'other' countries, processes that involve business partners are common. However, the differences are not significant ($H = 2.27$; $df = 2$; $p = 0.322$).

Table 4-1: Distribution of processes ($N_{NA} = 26$; $N_{EU} = 75$; $N_O = 29$) – Q33

Answers	ML	Rating (Scale Type 3)								
		Most			Some			A few		
		NA	EU	O	NA	EU	O	NA	EU	O
1 Department & 1 Person	—							12/46%	35/47%	13/45%
1 Department & > 1 Person	2			13/45%	11/43%	30/40%				
1 Company & > 1 Department	3	16/62%	52/69%	15/52%						
Other Companies	4.6				10/39%	29/39%	16/55%			
ML		3	3	3	2	2	4.6	1	2	1

Process timing ((Q35), (Q36)): For each of the rating levels of scale Type 3, Table 4-3 shows the most frequent answer alternative (i.e., the mode) concerning timing for each region. Again, the sparsely populated extreme ratings have been omitted. It becomes apparent that most processes in companies from Europe and the 'other' countries have a run time that is measured in days and are executed several times a day. *Long-running processes* whose run time and execution frequency are measured in weeks are most common in North America.

Table 4-2: Statistics for an average process - Q34

Please estimate the number of...	Minimum			Maximum			μ			σ			N/na		
	NA	E	O	NA	E	O	NA	E	O	NA	E	O	NA	E	O
Involved persons from the same department	1	1	3	50	55	10	9.72	5.44	4.95	13.65	9.11	0.50	26/8	75/43	29/18
Involved departments	2	1	1	10	8	18	3.94	3.24	4.50	2.00	110.27	0.24	26/9	75/38	29/16
Other companies involved	1	0	0	5	8	3	2.35	1.43	1.39	1.23	40.10	0.09	26/12	75/45	29/20
Software applications involved	1	1	1	15	15	11	4.13	4.14	4.13	3.33	144.95	0.02	26/11	75/38	29/17
Activities	3	6	3	120	60	30	25.79	16.10	10.56	30.83	491.01	0.02	26/13	75/43	29/20

Table 4-3: Timing of processes according to modes - Q35, Q36

Question	Rating (Scale Type 3)									N/na		
	Most			Some			A few					
	NA	EU	O	NA	EU	O	NA	EU	O	NA	EU	O
Measure of average process run time (Q35)	In days (10)	In days (29)	In days (15)	In weeks (13) In months (10)	In weeks (27)	In weeks (9)	In years (10)	In months (19)	In years (9); In months (7)	25/1	59/16	21/8
c_i / N	40.0 %	49.2 %	71.4 %	52.0 %	45.8 %	42.9 %	40.0 %	32.2 %	42.9 %			
Execution frequencies of processes (Q36)	Several times a day (12)	Several times a day (33)	Several times a day (14)	Several times per: week (19), month (13), year (11)	Several times per: week (30), month (29)	Several times per: month (14), week (9)	—	Several times a year (27)	Several times a year (13)	25/1	63/12	23/6
c_i / N	48.0 %	52.4 %	60.9 %	76.0 %	47.6 %	60.9 %	—	42.9 %	56.5 %			

The following questions discuss the nature of processes from the points of view of *analysis* (process scope (Q15), typical processes (Q13), process goals (Q25)), *process execution* (triggers (Q17), involved software applications (Q18)) as well as *process monitoring and improvement* (frequency of process changes (Q27); amount (Q28), impact (Q29) and reasons for process change (Q30) as well as methods for coping with process change (Q31)).

Process scope (Q15): By percentage (see Table 4-4), most processes in companies from North America and 'other' countries are related to software integration and data transformation, followed by system development as well as products. In Europe, most processes deal with products; administration and customer contact are the next important scopes of processes. The regional differences are not significant (χ^2_{ma} = 16.15; df = 12; p = 0.184).

Table 4-4: Process scope per region (N_{NA} = 26; N_{EU} = 71; N_O = 28) - Q15

Answers	ML	Count (c_i)			Percentage ($c_i / \Sigma c_i$)		
		NA	EU	O	NA	EU	O
Systems integration, data transformation	3	17	31	18	22.4 %	14.0 %	21.7 %
System development	–	16	34	15	21.1 %	15.4 %	18.1 %
Administration	3	14	43	14	18.4 %	19.5 %	16.9 %
A product of our company	3	14	49	15	18.4 %	22.2 %	18.1 %
Customer contact	3	10	42	15	13.2 %	19.0 %	18.1 %
Emergency procedure	3	5	22	6	6.6 %	10.0 %	7.2 %
Total		76	221	83	100.0 %	100.0 %	100.0 %

In all regions most representatives who filled in the questionnaire work in IT departments (see Table 3-2), so the dominance of IT-related processes in Table 4-4 is not surprising. However, Table 4-5 shows that within the IT departments processes are fairly equally associated with all scopes suggested as answer alternatives. Overall, from the point of view of the departments, most processes deal with the companies' products, followed by administration or customer contact (see Table 4-5). The differences between the departments are significant (χ^2_{ma} = 59.23; df = 24; p = 0.000), but the result of the modified Pearson chi-square test might be affected by the low cell counts.

Table 4-5: Process scope per department (N_{IT} = 86; N_{BPM} = 38; N_{CO} = 21; N_{FA} = 13) - Q15**

Answers	Count (c_i)				Percentage ($c_i / \Sigma c_i$)			
	IT	BPM	CO	FA	IT	BPM	CO	FA
Systems Integration, data transformation	53	21	7	4	19.0 %	15.3 %	10.8 %	12.9 %
Systems development	55	18	9	4	19.7 %	13.1 %	13.8 %	12.9 %
Administration	50	26	15	8	17.9 %	19.0 %	23.1 %	25.8 %
A product of our company	48	32	16	9	17.2 %	23.4 %	24.6 %	29.0 %
Customer contact	49	29	12	5	17.6 %	21.2 %	18.5 %	16.1 %
Emergency procedure	24	11	6	1	8.6 %	8.0 %	9.2 %	3.2 %
Total	279	137	65	31	100.0 %	100.0 %	100.0 %	100.0 %

Sample processes (Q13): To check whether the understanding of what constitutes a business process is consistent among the companies, we asked the participants (as an open text question) to freely list at least one title or short description of a typical process. Having obtained Σc_o =261 short descriptions, we clustered similar answers, see Table 4-6. Ordered by decreasing frequency, product-related and customer-related processes (e.g., order-to-pay, purchase-to-pay, fulfil order), processes related to software development (especially in companies from 'other' countries) as well as support processes (project management, incident management, human resource issues) were mentioned.

Table 4-6: Typical process descriptions per region (N_{NA} = 26; N_{EU} = 75; N_O = 29) – Q13

Answers (generalized and grouped)	Count (c_i)			Percentage ($c_i / \Sigma c_i$)		
	NA	EU	O	NA	EU	O
Order-to-pay	6	7	3	10.7 %	4.4 %	7.0 %
Purchase-to-pay	5	10	1	9.0 %	6.3 %	2.0 %
Project management related processes	3	5	1	5.4 %	3.1 %	2.0 %
Approval processes	3	1	1	5.4 %	1.0 %	2.0 %
Fulfil order, service	3	5	3	5.4 %	3.1 %	7.0 %
Incident management	2	5	2	3.5 %	3.1 %	4.0 %
Development processes, software, systems,	2	3	7	3.5 %	2.0 %	16.0 %
Change management	2	4	1	3.5 %	1.0 %	2.0 %
Human resources issues	2	6	1	3.5 %	1.0 %	2.0 %
Service request management related processes	2	2	1	3.5 %	1.3 %	2.0 %
Financial transactions	2	6	4	3.5 %	4.0 %	9.0 %
Production	1	3	1	2.0 %	2.0 %	2.0 %
Claims, complaints handling	1	3	1	2.0 %	2.0 %	2.0 %
Add a new customer	1	3	0	2.0 %	2.0 %	0.0 %
Loan, credit origination	1	1	1	2.0 %	1.0 %	2.0 %
Accounting related processes	0	8	0	0.0 %	5.0 %	0.0 %
Sales, sell product	0	5	0	0.0 %	3.1 %	0.0 %
Customer Relationship Management (CRM)	0	4	0	0.0 %	3.0 %	0.0 %
Support processes	0	4	0	0.0 %	3.0 %	0.0 %
Supply Chain Management (SCM)	0	3	1	0.0 %	2.0 %	2.0 %
Innovation processes (product)	0	3	0	0.0 %	2.0 %	0.0 %
Invoice processing	0	3	0	0.0 %	2.0 %	0.0 %
Demand management processes	0	3	0	0.0 %	2.0 %	0.0 %
Capture order, deal	0	2	0	0.0 %	1.3 %	0.0 %
Answer customer questions	0	2	1	0.0 %	1.3 %	2.0 %
Document management	0	2	0	0.0 %	1.3 %	0.0 %
Other different ones....	20	57	15	35.1 %	36.7 %	35.0 %
Total	56	160	45	100.0 %	100.0 %	100.0 %

Process goals (Q25): For this free text question concerning the process goals we obtained 127 answers, which were difficult to group. In total, timing goals were the most frequently mentioned goal category (c_o =10). Examples of timing goals are the reduction of cycle time, delays and waiting times. Timing goals were followed by customer satisfaction (c_o = 8) and quality-related goals (c_o = 7). Other named goals included the resolution of problems (c_o = 6) as well as the reduction of error rates (c_o = 5).

Process triggers (Q17): The most typical *trigger* of processes or activities is information sent from business partners in European companies and timing (e.g. deadlines or start dates that are reached; regular intervals such as every week) in companies from North America and the 'other' countries (see Table 4-7). The importance of information from business partners in Europe differs significantly from its importance in the other regions (H = 8.46; df = 2; p = 0.015). The differences in the ratings of signals are also significant (H = 6.93; df = 2; p = 0.031). The differences for all other answer alternatives are not significant.

Table 4-7: Triggers of processes per region (N_{NA} = 26; N_{EU} = 75; N_O = 29) - Q17(**)

Answer (Rating scale type 3)	μ			σ			Rank		
	NA	EU	O	NA	EU	O	NA	EU	O
Timing (date, regular intervals)	2.54	2.89	2.59	0.86	0.95	0.73	1	3	1
Company internal information	2.58	2.57	2.66	0.70	0.86	0.94	2	2	2
Human judgment and intervention	2.69	2.95	2.69	0.55	0.87	0.71	3	4	3
State of process or task	2.88	3.20	2.83	0.86	0.94	0.66	4	5	4
Information sent from business partners**	3.12	2.49	3.00	0.82	0.78	0.89	5	1	5
Deviations from targets or failures	3.58	3.52	3.14	0.76	1.01	0.79	6	6	6
Signals from machines and sensors**	3.96	4.01	3.59	0.87	0.81	0.68	7	7	7

Per department (see Table 4-9), timing ranks only third as a process trigger. Instead, information of any kind is the most important trigger. IT departments and departments for company organization focus on internal information, followed by information from business partners; for BPM departments as well as functional areas the order is reversed. However, these differences are statistically not significant.

Process enactment (Q18): In each region (see Table 4-8), databases and data warehouses are the *applications* used most often during process execution, followed by office software, ERP and CRM systems. BPM suites are rarely used, yet most often in Europe. The differences are not significant (χ^2_{ma} = 27.19; df = 28; p = 0.508), but the validity of the modified Pearson chi-square test is affected by the unbalanced cell counts.

Table 4-8: Applications involved in process execution per region (N_{NA} = 26; N_{EU} = 74; N_O = 28) - Q18

Answers	ML	Count (c_i)			Percentage ($c_i / \Sigma c_i$)		
		NA	EU	O	NA	EU	O
Database(s), data warehouse(s)	3	21	46	20	12.3 %	11.2 %	12.3 %
Office software	1	18	43	18	10.5 %	10.4 %	11.0 %
Enterprise resource planning system(s)	4	17	43	19	9.9 %	10.4 %	11.7 %
Procurement system(s)	4	16	32	15	9.4 %	7.8 %	9.2 %
Content management system(s)	—	16	31	9	9.4 %	7.5 %	5.5 %
Customer relationship management system(s)	4	14	45	17	8.2 %	10.9 %	10.4 %
Integration software, middleware	3	14	38	14	8.2 %	9.2 %	8.6 %
Supply chain management system(s)	4.6	13	28	14	7.6 %	6.8 %	8.6 %
Product data management system(s)	3	12	27	11	7.0 %	6.6 %	6.7 %
Production data acquisition	4	9	14	6	5.3 %	3.4 %	3.7 %
Application software at business partners	4.6	8	23	7	4.7 %	5.6 %	4.3 %
BPM suites	3.8	6	28	7	3.5 %	6.8 %	4.3 %
Educational software	—	4	8	6	2.3 %	1.9 %	3.7 %
No software	—	3	6	0	1.8 %	1.5 %	0.0 %
Total		171	412	166	100.0 %	100.0 %	100.0 %

When analyzing the responses to Question (Q18) per department (Table 4-10), databases and data warehouse(s) remain the most needed software applications for participants from IT departments, whereas representatives of departments for company organization selected ERP systems more often. In functional areas, ERP systems are as much involved in process execution as databases. Interestingly, representatives from BPM departments declared office software to be the most important application type for process execution. Irrespective of the representatives' departmental affiliation, the prevalence of BPM suites is rather low. The overall differences in software usage are significant (χ^2_{ma} = 101.30; df = 56; p = 0.000).

Table 4-9: Triggers of processes per department ($N_{IT} = 88$; $N_{BPM} = 38$; $N_{CO} = 22$; $N_{FA} = 13$) - Q17

Answer (Rating scale type 3)	μ				σ				Rank			
	IT	BPM	CO	FA	IT	BPM	CO	FA	IT	BPM	CO	FA
Timing (date, regular intervals)	2.90	2.82	2.68	2.88	0.83	0.96	1.04	0.96	4	3	3	3
Company internal information	2.67	2.53	2.09	2.81	0.84	0.86	0.75	0.91	1	2	1	2
Human judgment and intervention	2.77	2.82	2.91	3.19	0.74	0.93	0.87	0.83	3	3	4	5
State of process or task	3.14	3.11	3.18	2.94	0.89	0.95	1.01	0.57	5	4	5	4
Information sent from business partners	2.69	2.50	2.64	2.63	0.82	0.76	0.90	0.89	2	1	2	1
Deviations from targets or failures	3.42	3.58	3.73	3.50	0.84	0.95	1.20	0.97	6	5	6	6
Signals from machines and sensors	3.84	3.89	4.00	4.19	0.80	0.83	0.76	0.75	7	6	7	7

Table 4-10: Applications involved in process execution per department ($N_{IT} = 88$; $N_{BPM} = 38$; $N_{CO} = 22$; $N_{FA} = 16$) - Q18**

Answers	Count (c_i)				Percentage ($c_i / \Sigma c_i$)			
	IT	BPM	CO	FA	IT	BPM	CO	FA
Database(s), data warehouse(s)	66	21	10	9	11.8 %	10.1 %	8.7 %	13.8 %
Office software	55	24	13	7	9.8 %	11.6 %	11.3 %	10.8 %
Enterprise resource planning system(s)	62	19	17	9	11.1 %	9.2 %	14.8 %	13.8 %
Procurement system(s)	49	20	12	5	8.8 %	9.7 %	10.4 %	7.7 %
Content management system(s)	43	18	10	3	7.7 %	8.7 %	8.7 %	4.6 %
Customer relationship management system(s)	59	16	10	3	10.6 %	7.7 %	8.7 %	4.6 %
Integration software, middleware	52	12	6	6	9.3 %	5.8 %	5.2 %	9.2 %
Supply chain management system(s)	44	15	7	3	7.9 %	7.2 %	6.1 %	4.6 %
Product data management system(s)	37	20	7	6	6.6 %	9.7 %	6.1 %	9.2 %
Production data acquisition	22	15	6	2	3.9 %	7.2 %	5.2 %	3.1 %
Application software at business partners	27	12	7	4	4.8 %	5.8 %	6.1 %	6.2 %
BPM suites	27	7	6	3	4.8 %	3.4 %	5.2 %	4.6 %
Educational software	14	5	2	1	2.5 %	2.4 %	1.7 %	1.5 %
No software	2	3	2	4	0.4 %	1.4 %	1.7 %	6.2 %
Total	559	207	115	65	100.0 %	100.0 %	100.0 %	100.0 %

Process monitoring and improvement (Q27): The business processes in the participating companies are quite *stable* (see Table 4-11). They are changed rarely in the companies from North America and the 'other' countries and yearly in the European companies. Altogether, processes of the companies from the 'other' countries seem to be slightly more flexible since the percentages of monthly and weekly changes are higher than in the other regions. The differences between the regions are not significant ($\chi^2_{ma} = 9.02$; df = 12; p=0.701); however, the validity of the test is restricted by the empty cells.

Table 4-11: Frequency of process change per region ($N_{NA} = 24$; $N_{EU} = 64$; $N_O = 23$) - Q27

Answer	ML	Count (c_i)			Percentage ($c_i / \Sigma c_i$)		
		NA	EU	O	NA	EU	O
Yearly	2	8	25	6	33.3 %	39.1 %	26.1 %
Rarely	1	8	14	8	33.3 %	21.9 %	34.8 %
Quarterly	2	5	19	5	20.8 %	29.7 %	21.7 %
Weekly	3	2	1	1	8.3 %	1.6 %	4.3 %
Monthly	3	1	4	3	4.2 %	6.3 %	13.0 %
Daily	5	0	0	0	0.0 %	0.0 %	0.0 %
In each execution	5	0	1	0	0.0 %	1.6 %	0.0 %
Total		24	64	23	100.0 %	100.0 %	100.0 %

Process change: The *amount of change* (Q28) is situation-specific; this answer was uniformly given by companies from all regions (see Table 4-12) and participants from any department (see Table 4-13). In general, minor changes prevail (both per region and per department). Major changes are most common in companies from the 'other' countries. The regional differences are significant ($\chi^2_{ma} = 14.67$; df = 6; p = 0.023), whilst the departmental ones are not ($\chi^2_{ma} = 13.36$; df = 12; p = 0.343). The test's validity might be affected by the unbalanced cell counts.

Table 4-12: Amount of process change per region ($N_{NA} = 26$; $N_{EU} = 75$; $N_O = 29$) - Q28**

Answers	Count (c_i)			Percentage ($c_i / \Sigma c_i$)		
	NA	EU	O	NA	EU	O
It depends	16	53	23	51.6 %	64.6 %	67.6 %
Minor change	14	28	7	45.2 %	34.1 %	20.6 %
Major change	1	1	4	3.2 %	1.2 %	11.8 %
Total	31	82	34	100.0 %	100.0 %	100.0 %

Table 4-13: Amount of process change per department ($N_{IT} = 88$; $N_{BPM} = 38$; $N_{CO} = 22$; $N_{FA} = 16$) - Q28

Answers	Count (c_i)				Percentage ($c_i / \Sigma c_i$)			
	IT	BPM	CO	FA	IT	BPM	CO	FA
It depends	60	31	17	12	59.4 %	70.5 %	63.0 %	66.7 %
Minor change	36	11	9	6	35.6 %	25.0 %	33.3 %	33.3 %
Major change	5	2	1	0	5.0 %	4.5 %	3.7 %	0.0 %
Total	101	44	27	18	100.0 %	100.0 %	100.0 %	100.0 %

Mostly, *process change* has long-lasting *impact* (Q29) as it affects all future executions of the process, see Table 4-14. In the opinion of the departments, it depends on the situation whether or not a change is valid for all or just a few process executions, see Table 4-15. Changes that affect just the current process execution are only common in functional areas. Neither the regional differences ($\chi^2_{ma} = 1.00$; df = 4; p = 0.905) nor the differences between the departments ($\chi^2_{ma} = 9.054$; df = 8; p = 0.338) are significant.

Table 4-14: Impact of process change per region ($N_{NA} = 26$; $N_{EU} = 75$; $N_O = 29$) - Q29

Answer	Count (c_i)			Percentage ($c_i / \Sigma c_i$)		
	NA	EU	O	NA	EU	O
All future executions	13	39	13	50.0 %	52.0 %	44.8 %
It depends	13	33	15	50.0 %	44.0 %	51.7 %
Only current execution	0	3	1	0.0 %	4.0 %	3.4 %
Total	26	75	29	100.0 %	100.0 %	100.0 %

Table 4-15: Impact of process change per department ($N_{IT} = 88$; $N_{BPM} = 38$; $N_{CO} = 22$; $N_{FA} = 16$) - Q29

Answers	Count (c_i)				Percentage ($c_i / \Sigma c_i$)			
	IT	BPM	CO	FA	IT	BPM	CO	FA
All future executions	38	18	13	1	43.2 %	47.4 %	59.1 %	6.3 %
It depends	47	20	9	10	53.4 %	52.6 %	40.9 %	62.5 %
Only current execution	3	0	0	5	3.4 %	0.0 %	0.0 %	31.3 %
Total	88	38	22	16	100.0 %	100.0 %	100.0 %	100.0 %

Reasons for process change (Q30): Process changes occur mainly in line with the evolving business (North America, Europe) or are forced by the environment ('other' countries), see Table 4-16. Evaluating the answers to Question (Q30) per department leads to the same result (see Table 4-17). Here, representatives from departments for company organization in particular attribute process change to company-external forces (e.g. changed laws or standards from business partners). Deviations from planned values are commonly the third most important reason for changing a process. The regions differ significantly in the reasons for process change ($\chi^2_{ma} = 26.87$; df = 10; p = 0.003), whereas the differences among the departments are not significant ($\chi^2_{ma} = 27.83$; df = 20; p = 0.113).

Table 4-16: Reasons for process change per region ($N_{NA} = 26$; $N_{EU} = 75$; $N_O = 29$) - Q30**

Answers	ML	Count (c_i)			Percentage ($c_i / \Sigma c_i$)		
		NA	EU	O	NA	EU	O
In line with the evolving business	5.1	26	69	20	44.8 %	41.1 %	31.3 %
Forced by environment	3	14	57	21	24.1 %	33.9 %	32.8 %
Deviations from planned values	3	9	28	15	15.5 %	16.7 %	23.4 %
Internal disruptions	3	9	12	7	15.5 %	7.1 %	10.9 %
Next task is always determined ad hoc	1	0	2	1	0.0 %	1.2 %	1.6 %
Total		58	168	64	100.0 %	100.0 %	100.0 %

Table 4-17: Reasons for process change per department ($N_{IT} = 88$; $N_{BPM} = 38$; $N_{CO} = 22$; $N_{FA} = 16$) – Q30

Answers	Count (c_i)				Percentage ($c_i / \Sigma c_i$)			
	IT	BPM	CO	FA	IT	BPM	CO	FA
In line with the evolving business	79	36	19	12	40.5 %	37.1 %	37.3 %	40.0 %
Forced by environment	61	31	21	9	31.3 %	32.0 %	41.2 %	30.0 %
Deviations from planned values	34	16	8	6	17.4 %	16.5 %	15.7 %	20.0 %
Internal disruptions	18	12	3	3	9.2 %	12.4 %	5.9 %	10.0 %
Next task is always determined ad hoc	3	2	0	0	1.5 %	2.1 %	0.0 %	0.0 %
Total	195	97	51	30	100.0 %	100.0 %	100.0 %	100.0 %

Coping with process change (Q31): Companies from all regions (see Table 4-18) and representatives from all departments (see Table 4-19) preferably cope with process change by applying change mechanisms. Predefined process variants are widely used in companies from 'other' countries and in IT departments. Task postponement seems to be typical for North American companies and functional areas. The low cell counts and empty cells preclude the use of the modified Pearson chi-square test.

Table 4-18: Coping with process change per region ($N_{NA} = 22$; $N_{EU} = 55$; $N_O = 19$) - Q31

Answer	ML	Count (c_i)			Percentage ($c_i / \Sigma c_i$)		
		NA	EU	O	NA	EU	O
By applying change mechanisms	3	17	45	14	77.3 %	81.8 %	73.7 %
By postponing selection of tasks	5	2	3	0	9.1 %	5.5 %	0.0 %
By having predefined process variants	3	1	2	3	4.5 %	3.6 %	15.8 %
None of the above	—	2	5	2	9.1 %	6.7 %	10.5 %
Total		22	55	19	100.0 %	100.0 %	100.0 %

Table 4-19: Coping with process change per department ($N_{IT} = 65$; $N_{BPM} = 26$; $N_{CO} = 16$; $N_{FA} = 12$) - Q31

Answers	Count (c_i)				Percentage ($c_i / \Sigma c_i$)			
	IT	BPM	CO	FA	IT	BPM	CO	FA
By applying change mechanisms	48	22	15	8	54.5 %	57.9 %	68.2 %	50.0 %
By postponing selection of tasks	3	1	0	2	3.4 %	2.6 %	0.0 %	12.5 %
By having predefined process variants	6	0	0	0	6.8 %	0.0 %	0.0 %	0.0 %
None of the above	8	3	1	2	9.1 %	0.0 %	4.5 %	12.5 %
Total	65	26	16	12	100.0 %	100.0 %	100.0 %	100.0 %

We also inquired after the nature of change mechanisms (Q32), e.g. whether insertions, deletions and replacements of tasks or flow modifications were preferred. However, the number of missing values was too high to yield representative results for this question.

Altogether, current business processes can be described as being largely internal, spanning about four departments, whilst still maintaining connections to one or two business partners. Most business processes are related to a company's products or IT and are quite stable. Current business processes are not long-running, as their run times and execution frequencies are mostly measured in days. The execution of business processes relies on numerous, heterogeneous software applications; BPM systems and BPM suites are not as widespread as could have been expected. Hence the particular requirements for BPM software should be investigated in more detail: this is done in the next section.

4.3 Software in Business Process Management

According to Question Q18 (Table 4-8 and Table 4-10), BPM suites currently play a subordinate role in the execution of business processes. However, *BPM suites* are just the most recent and most sophisticated type of software for BPM, enabling process description, analysis and automation (see Section 1). *BPM tools*, which support at least process modelling (and often also model analysis), and *BPM systems* that automate processes (e.g., by integrating software applications along the process) are precursors of BPM suites. The distinction between these types of BPM software is becoming increasingly blurred.

It was the goal of this investigation to dig deeper into the requirements for BPM software. For this reason we asked the companies about their current software usage (which BPM tool/system (Q11) and why it was chosen (Q12)) and the functionalities or qualities, which the companies expect from BPM software in general (Q8) and for supporting process enactment (Q9) as well as monitoring (Q10) in particular.

Currently used software for BPM (Q11): Describing business processes is the lowest requirement for software to be called a 'BPM tool'. Both textual and graphical descriptions can occur (see also Section 4.4). General office software such as Microsoft Visio and Microsoft Word makes up the dominating BPM tool in all regions (see Table 4-20) and departments (see Table 4-21). Even in IT departments Microsoft Visio is clearly preferred to, for example, IBM Websphere (see Table 4-21). The convenience of Microsoft Visio for IT departments is grounded in the Visio stencils, which not only allow the definition of shapes, particular attributes and model validation routines, but can also by linked to software development tools and databases in order to support functionalities far beyond (process) modelling.

Table 4-20: Currently used BPM software per region (N_{NA} = 25; N_{EU} = 67; N_O = 27) - Q11**

Answers	ML	Count (c_i)			Percentage ($c_i / \Sigma c_i$)		
		NA	EU	O	NA	EU	O
Microsoft Visio	2.7	22	41	15	36.1 %	29.1 %	22.4 %
Microsoft Word	2	15	27	18	24.6 %	19.1 %	26.9 %
SAP R/3 or mySAP ECC	3.8	8	21	10	13.1 %	14.9 %	14.9 %
IBM Websphere BPM	3.8	6	9	8	9.8 %	6.4 %	11.9 %
In-house solution	2.5	4	11	9	6.6 %	7.8 %	13.4 %
ARIS Toolset	3.8	3	22	4	4.9 %	15.6 %	6.0 %
Oracle BPM	3.8	2	1	1	3.3 %	0.7 %	1.5 %
iGrafx Suite	2.7	2	1	1	3.3 %	0.7 %	1.5 %
Intalio BPMS	3.8	1	1	0	1.6 %	1.6 %	0.0 %
TIBCO iProcess Suite	3.8	0	3	2	0.0 %	2.1 %	3.0 %
ADONIS	2.7	0	3	0	0.0 %	2.1 %	0.0 %
Ibo Prometheus Suite, Semtalk	2.7	0	2	0	0.0 %	1.4 %	0.0 %
Total		61	141	67	100.0 %	100.0 %	100.0 %

In companies from North America and the 'other' countries, the EPR system from SAP, which includes a workflow component, is the third most important application to describe and manage processes, whereas in Europe the ARIS toolset, a particular BPM suite, is used more often. It is mainly BPM departments that rely on the ARIS toolset, but it is also used in IT departments (see Table 4-21).

Table 4-21: Currently used BPM software per department (N_{IT} = 86; N_{BPM} = 33; N_{CO} = 16; N_{FA} = 16) - Q11**

Answers	Count (c_i)				Percentage ($c_i / \Sigma c_i$)			
	IT	BPM	CO	FA	IT	BPM	CO	FA
Microsoft Visio	60	20	9	9	29.1 %	31.3 %	27.3 %	27.3 %
Microsoft Word	46	10	6	8	22.3 %	15.6 %	18.2 %	24.2 %
ARIS Toolset	26	10	3	1	12.6 %	15.6 %	9.1 %	3.0 %
SAP R/3 or mySAP ECC	32	6	4	3	15.5 %	9.4 %	12.1 %	9.1 %
IBM Websphere BPM	19	7	2	1	9.2 %	10.9 %	6.1 %	3.0 %
In-house solution	14	4	4	8	6.8 %	6.3 %	12.1 %	24.2 %
TIBCO iProcess Suite	4	1	1	0	1.9 %	1.6 %	3.0 %	0.0 %
iGrafx Suite, Oracle	2	2	0	2	1.0 %	3.1 %	0.0 %	6.1 %
Intalio BPMS	1	2	1	1	0.5 %	3.1 %	3.0 %	3.0 %
ADONIS	1	1	2	0	0.5 %	1.6 %	6.1 %	0.0 %
Prometheus Suite	1	1	0	0	0.5 %	1.6 %	0.0 %	0.0 %
Semtalk	0	0	1	0	0.0 %	0.0 %	3.0 %	0.0 %
Total	206	64	33	33	100.0 %	100.0 %	100.0 %	100.0 %

On a global scale, IBM Websphere BPM is the dominating BPM suite; however, in-house solutions are almost as or even more common (see Table 4-20). As open answers, mainly other Microsoft tools (EXCEL, PowerPoint, SharePoint) as well as NIMBUS control software, BizAgi Process Modeler and CASEwise were mentioned. The regional differences (χ^2_{ma} = 37.03; df = 24; p = 0.04) and the differences among the departments (χ^2_{ma} = 92.90; df = 48; p = 0.00) are statistically significant, with minor restrictions on the validity of the test because of the unbalanced and partially low cell counts.

BPM software selection (Q12): Unanimously, the companies selected their BPM software because of its functionalities and qualities – see Table 4-22 and Table 4-23. In North American companies (see Table 4-22) as well as for IT and BPM departments (see Table 4-23), the tool's price is the second most important criterion, whereas European companies as well as departments for company organization or functional areas put more emphasis on support. Whether or not the BPM tool was already available in the company was almost irrelevant. Only the regional differences in the ratings of 'functionalities and qualities' are significant (H = 7.72; df = 2; p = 0.021). The differences between the departments concerning 'functionalities and qualities' are significant at the α = 0.1 level (H = 8.34; df = 4; p = 0.080).

Table 4-22: Decision criteria for BPM software selection per region (N_{NA} = 26; N_{EU} = 75; N_O = 29) - Q12 (**)

Answer	μ			σ			Rank		
	NA	EU	O	NA	EU	O	NA	EU	O
Functionalities and qualities**	2.31	1.60	1.72	1.72	1.37	1.33	1	1	1
Pricing	2.54	3.17	2.93	1.39	1.29	1.41	2	3	2
Support	3.00	3.08	2.93	1.10	1.30	1.07	3	2	2
Vendor image	3.31	3.37	3.69	1.23	0.91	1.04	4	4	4
Availability	3.85	3.77	3.72	1.12	1.15	1.28	5	5	5

Table 4-23: Decision criteria for BPM software selection per department ($N_{IT} = 88$; $N_{BPM} = 38$; $N_{CO} = 22$; $N_{FA} = 16$) - Q12(*)

Answer	μ				σ				Rank			
	IT	BPM	CO	FA	IT	BPM	CO	FA	IT	BPM	CO	FA
Functionalities and qualities*	1.80	1.37	1.55	2.25	1.46	1.10	1.18	1.81	1	1	1	1
Pricing	2.94	3.00	3.27	3.06	1.38	1.27	1.42	1.29	2	2	3	3
Support	3.07	3.32	3.09	2.81	1.18	1.09	1.34	1.11	3	3	2	2
Vendor image	3.42	3.32	3.27	3.56	1.04	0.84	0.83	1.15	4	3	3	5
Availability	3.77	4.00	3.82	3.31	1.16	1.25	1.22	1.45	5	4	4	4

Requirements for BPM software (Q8): The most important criterion in order to select particular BPM software was investigated in more detail by asking the companies to assess the importance of a list of functionalities and qualities. In all regions (see Table 4-24) the most important quality of software for BPM is *usability*, i.e. human-computer interaction that is obvious, easy to learn and efficient (it does not take too much time to accomplish a task). In companies from Europe and the 'other' countries, usability is followed by modelling capabilities, whereas in North America report generation is more crucial (see Table 4-24). Software integration is placed third in companies from North America and the 'other' countries and fifth in European companies. The adaptability of the process modelling language provided by the tool, correctness proofs and syntax checks for process models as well as support for different notations is almost irrelevant. Only the regional differences in the rating of modelling capabilities are statistically significant ($H = 13.60$; $df = 2$; $p = 0.001$).

When analyzing the answers to question (Q8) per department, usability stays in first place (see Table 4-25). For functional areas, the capability of integrating software is the second most important functionality of BPM tools, for all other departments report generation capabilities come second. Only for IT departments, modelling capabilities take third place; in other departments they are less appreciated. The third place is assigned to process monitoring in the functional areas and to alignment with standards in BPM and CO departments. The differences in the ratings of modelling capabilities ($H = 9.94$; $df = 4$; $p = 0.041$), report generation ($H = 12.39$; $df = 4$; $p = 0.015$) and process monitoring ($H = 9.87$; $df = 4$; $p = 0.043$) are significant.

Figure 4-2 visualizes the variation in the required BPM software functionalities and qualities per department; their differences are quite obvious. The most frequent requirements entered as free text answers to Question (Q8) were support for multi-user environments, support for process model versioning and open source software.

Table 4-24: Important functionalities and qualities for BPM tools per region ($N_{NA} = 26$; $N_{EU} = 75$; $N_O = 29$) – Q8 (**)

Answer (Rating scale type 4)	μ			σ			Rank		
	NA	EU	O	NA	EU	O	NA	EU	O
Usability	1.62	1.40	1.62	0.90	0.68	0.82	1	1	1
Report generation	2.15	2.07	2.28	1.05	1.02	0.80	2	3	5
Modelling capabilities**	2.19	1.64	1.90	0.90	0.93	0.86	3	2	2
Software integration	2.19	2.15	2.00	0.94	1.05	0.93	3	5	3
Alignment to standards	2.27	2.13	2.24	0.87	0.92	1.09	4	4	4
Process execution	2.42	2.07	2.28	1.03	0.98	0.92	5	3	5
Process monitoring	2.46	2.15	2.31	0.95	1.06	1.00	6	5	6
Process simulation	2.50	2.49	2.28	0.91	0.98	0.96	7	6	5
Language adaptability	2.54	2.59	2.31	0.81	1.07	0.97	8	9	6
Correctness proofs	2.62	2.53	2.52	0.94	1.02	1.15	9	7	7
Syntax checks	2.73	2.56	2.83	0.83	0.95	1.28	10	8	9
Different notations/standards	2.73	2.71	2.76	0.92	1.01	1.15	11	10	8

Table 4-25: Important functionalities and qualities for BPM tools per department ($N_{IT} = 88$; $N_{BPM} = 38$; $N_{CO} = 22$; $N_{FA} = 16$) – Q8 (**)

Answer (Rating scale type 4)	μ				σ				Rank			
	IT	BPM	CO	FA	IT	BPM	CO	FA	IT	BPM	CO	FA
Usability	1.55	1.37	1.41	1.38	0.84	0.75	0.59	0.50	1	1	1	1
Report generation**	1.84	1.58	1.68	2.25	0.90	0.89	0.72	1.34	2	2	2	6
Modelling capabilities**	2.01	2.00	2.50	2.38	0.97	1.07	1.10	1.81	3	4	7	7
Software integration	2.18	2.13	2.32	1.50	1.02	1.07	1.04	0.52	4	7	5	2
Alignment to standards	2.19	1.95	2.23	2.56	0.97	0.96	0.69	1.21	5	3	3	8
Process execution	2.27	2.11	2.27	2.13	1.03	0.89	0.88	0.96	6	6	4	4
Process monitoring**	2.34	2.08	2.55	1.94	1.05	0.94	1.01	0.85	7	5	8	3
Process simulation	2.48	2.42	2.91	2.19	0.98	1.00	0.92	0.83	8	10	10	5
Language adaptability	2.56	2.39	2.50	2.69	0.98	0.92	1.01	1.35	9	9	7	9
Correctness proofs	2.58	2.32	2.64	2.88	1.03	0.87	0.90	1.50	10	8	9	11
Syntax checks	2.68	2.58	2.45	3.00	1.02	0.92	0.86	1.32	11	11	6	12
Different notations/ standards	2.69	2.68	2.95	2.81	1.00	1.04	1.01	1.33	12	12	11	10

Software is mainly needed in the phases 'process design', 'process enactment' and 'process monitoring' of the BPM life cycle. Modelling capabilities, adaptability of the process modelling language, correctness proofs and syntax checks for process models as well as support for different notations and standards (see Table 4-24 and Table 4-25) are software functionalities related to *process design*. Other requirements for this phase of the BPM life cycle are discussed in Section 4.4.

Process enactment (Q9): We asked the companies how they wished to be supported by software during process execution; the answers are shown in Table 4-26 per region and in Table 4-27 per department. Most companies want software to execute particular tasks, followed by task routing and information proving; automated process execution is not substantially required. This overall order of required software support for process execution pertains to all regions and departments. The minor differences in the ratings (Rating scale type 4) are not significant. For question (Q9B), which dealt with the necessity of human intervention during process enactment, we did not obtain enough responses to yield reliable results.

Table 4-26: Required kind of support for process execution per region– Q9

	Execution of tasks			Routing of tasks			Information providing			Automated process execution		
ML	1			3.8			1			3.8		
	NA	EU	O	NA	EU	O	NA	EU	O	NA	EU	O
N Counts	24	71	25	23	65	24	23	66	24	24	68	25
na Missing values	2	4	4	3	10	5	3	9	5	2	7	4
Mean (μ) – Scale 4	2.21	2.11	2.00	2.43	2.38	2.54	2.48	2.62	2.38	2.79	2.90	2.68
Std. deviation (σ)	0.72	0.84	0.76	0.73	0.82	0.93	0.67	1.09	0.97	0.83	0.85	0.90
Rank	1	1	1	2	2	3	3	3	2	4	4	4

In addition to the answer alternatives provided in the questionnaire, the companies frequently mentioned that software should support them during process enactment by sending alerts, by escalation features, by tracking the execution status and by showing bottlenecks. All of these requirements refer to process monitoring.

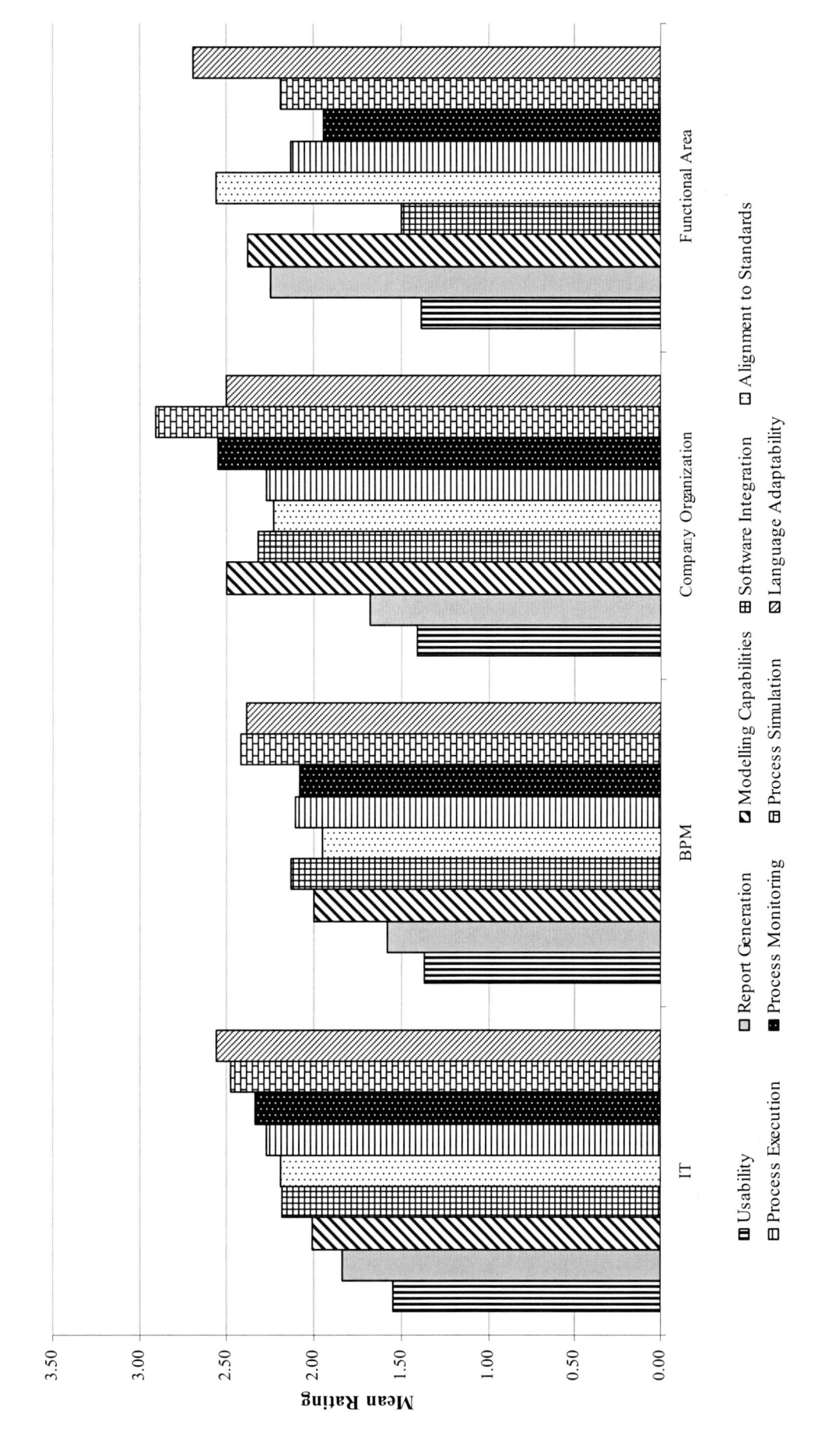

Figure 4-2: Important functionalities and qualities for BPM tools per department – Rating scale Type 4 ($N_{IT} = 88$; $N_{BPM} = 38$; $N_{CO} = 22$; $N_{FA} = 16$) – Q8 (**)

Table 4-27: Required kind of support for process execution per department- Q9

		Execution of Tasks			Routing of Tasks			Information Providing			Automated Process Execution		
		IT	BPM	CO	FA	IT	BPM	CO	FA	IT	BPM	CO	FA
N	Counts	81	36	20	15	76	33	20	14	77	35	20	13	78	34	19	15
na	Missing values	7	2	2	1	12	5	2	2	11	3	2	3	10	4	3	1
	Mean (μ)	1.99	2.17	2.25	2.13	2.51	2.21	2.35	2.21	2.55	2.57	2.45	2.62	2.76	2.94	3.00	2.87
	Std. deviation (σ)	0.78	1.00	0.64	0.52	0.77	0.89	0.99	0.80	1.03	1.01	1.15	0.65	0.84	1.01	0.75	0.83
	Rank	1	1	1	1	2	2	2	2	3	3	3	3	4	4	4	4

Process monitoring (Q10): In a separate question, the information the companies wish to monitor was explicitly inquired after. The results are shown in Table 4-28 per region and in Table 4-29 per department. The execution status is clearly the most important information to be monitored, followed by times and failures during process execution. Neither the regional differences (χ^2_{ma} = 16.58; df = 14; p=0.279) nor the differences between departments (χ^2_{ma} = 32.37; df = 28; p=0.260) are significant.

Table 4-28: Information wished to be monitored per region (N_{NA} = 26; N_{EU} = 74; N_O = 28) – Q10

Answers	ML	Count (c_i)			Percentage ($c_i / \Sigma c_i$)		
		NA	EU	O	NA	EU	O
Failures in process execution	3.7	24	51	22	23.5 %	19.9 %	21.6 %
Times	4.2	22	61	23	21.6 %	23.8 %	22.5 %
Execution status	3.7	21	65	24	20.6 %	25.4 %	23.5 %
Deviations from process model	3.7	18	37	10	17.6 %	14.5 %	9.8 %
Tasks' processors	3.7	7	17	7	6.9 %	6.6 %	6.9 %
Consumed material	4.2	6	13	8	5.9 %	5.1 %	7.8 %
Machines occupied	4.2	4	10	6	3.9 %	3.9 %	5.9 %
Nothing	1	0	2	2	0.0 %	0.8 %	2.0 %
Total		102	256	102	100.0 %	100.0 %	100.0 %

Table 4-29: Information wished to be monitored per department (N_{IT} = 88; N_{BPM} = 38; N_{CO} = 21; N_{FA} = 15) – Q10

Answers	Count (c_i)				Percentage ($c_i / \Sigma c_i$)			
	IT	BPM	CO	FA	IT	BPM	CO	FA
Failures in process execution	72	33	10	10	21.8 %	23.1 %	15.2 %	18.2 %
Times	73	32	17	14	22.1 %	22.4 %	25.8 %	25.5 %
Execution status	75	34	19	14	22.7 %	23.8 %	28.8 %	25.5 %
Deviations from process model	43	21	11	8	13.0 %	14.7 %	16.7 %	14.5 %
Tasks' processors	25	11	4	3	7.6 %	7.7 %	6.1 %	5.5 %
Consumed material	21	6	2	4	6.3 %	4.2 %	3.0 %	7.3 %
Machines occupied	18	5	3	2	5.4 %	3.5 %	4.5 %	3.6 %
Nothing	4	1	0	0	1.2 %	0.7 %	0.0 %	0.0 %
Total	331	143	66	55	100.0 %	100.0 %	100.0 %	100.0 %

4.4 Describing Business Processes

Modelling capabilities are among the top four requirements for BPM software (see Table 4-24). This section explores in more detail how companies proceed in describing their business processes (Questions (Q3), (Q16), (Q4)) and which concepts they need (Questions (Q19) to (Q22)).

Reasons for describing processes (Q5): As process modelling causes effort, it is not end in itself but is done for a reason. Hence the companies were asked why they describe their business processes. The phrase 'process description' was used with the intention not to jump to graphical process modelling, but also to allow other description styles (see question (Q4)). Figure 4-3 and Figure 4-4 summarize the results per department and per region. Both figures show that the reasons for describing processes are distinct.

Preparing *business process reengineering*, i.e. the redesign of business processes to increase their effectiveness and efficiency, is the most important reason for describing processes. This was stated by North American and European companies (see Table 4-30) as well as by representatives from all departments – except for company organization (see Table 4-31). In departments for company organization and in companies from the 'other'

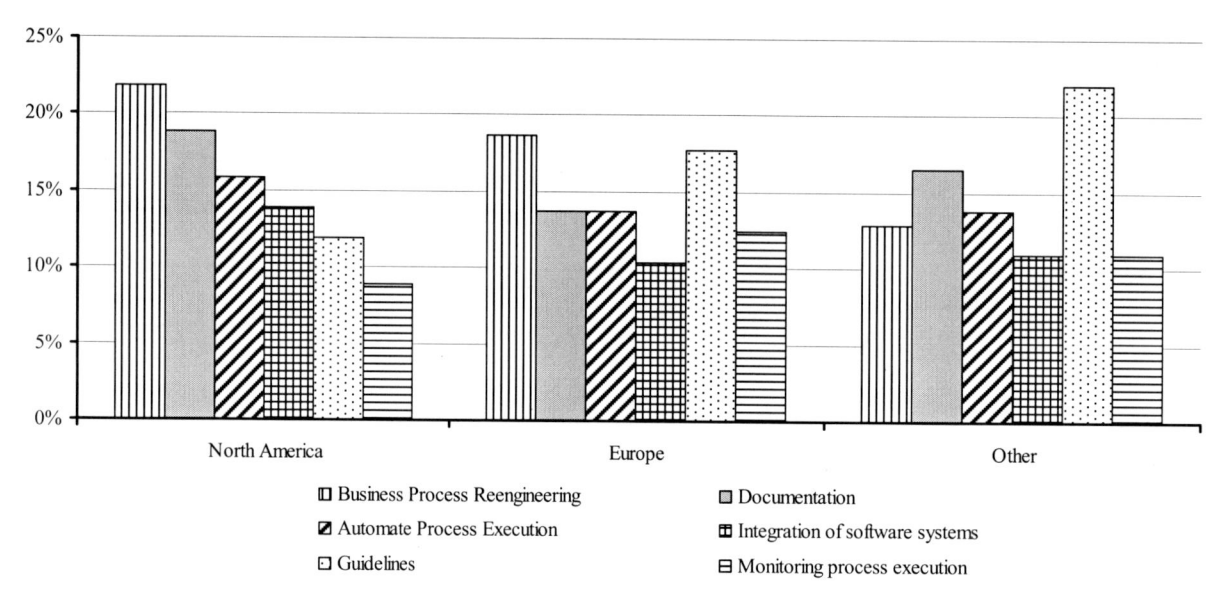

Figure 4-3: Reasons to describe processes per Region – Q5

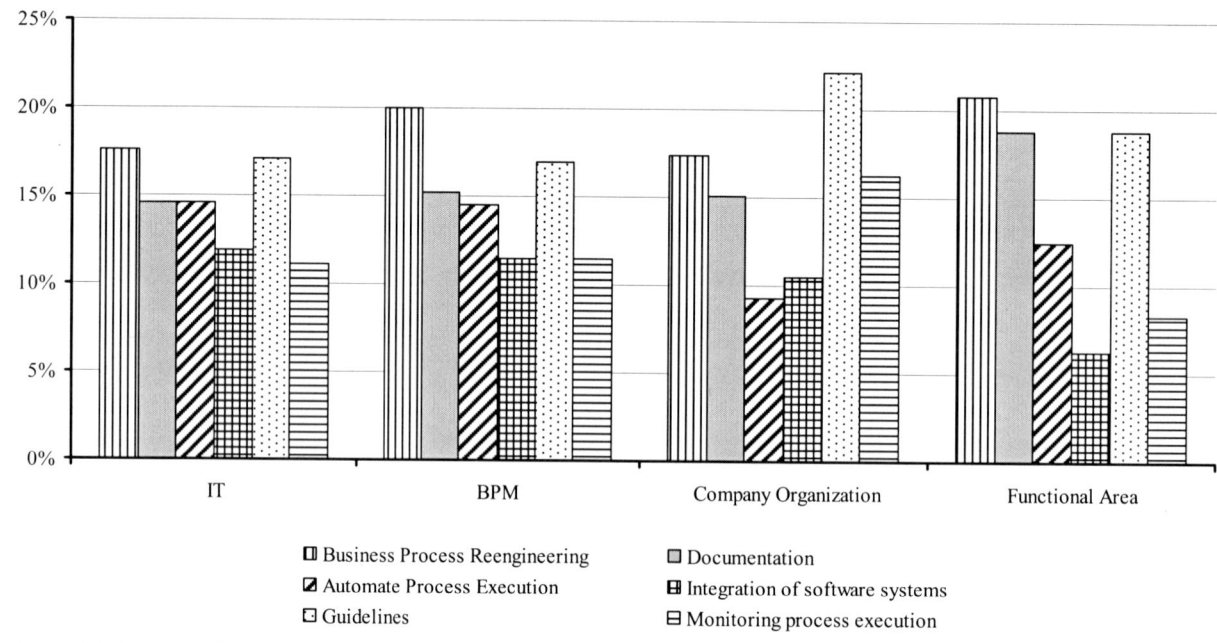

Figure 4-4: Reasons to describe processes per department – Q5

countries, processes are described mainly to have guidelines for the persons involved in process execution. After business process reengineering and having guidelines, the next important motives for process descriptions are documentation (of 'as-is' processes), the automation of process execution and software integration. The differences between the regions are significant (χ^2_{ma} = 25.49; df = 12; p=0.013), as opposed to the differences between the departments (χ^2_{ma} = 31.68; df = 24; p=0.135).

Not surprisingly, in departments for company organization, process automation is not a prominent driving force for process descriptions – however, software integration is nearly as important as in departments for IT and BPM (see Table 4-30). Of all the departments, company organization is the one that puts most emphasis on having process descriptions to monitor process execution – though this functionality was mostly appreciated by functional areas (see Table 4-25). Among the open answers to question (Q5), compliance was mentioned most frequently (c_o = 5) as an additional reason for describing processes.

Table 4-30: Reasons to describe processes per region ($N_{NA} = 26$; $N_{EU} = 75$; $N_O = 29$) – Q5**

Answers	ML	Count (c_i)			Percentage ($c_i / \Sigma c_i$)		
		NA	EU	O	NA	EU	O
Business process reengineering	5.1	22	56	14	21.8 %	18.7 %	12.8 %
Documentation	2	19	41	18	18.8 %	13.7 %	16.5 %
Automate process execution	3.8	16	41	15	15.8 %	13.7 %	13.8 %
Integration of software systems	3	14	31	12	13.9 %	10.4 %	11.0 %
Guidelines	2.7	12	53	24	11.9 %	17.7 %	22.0 %
Monitoring process execution	3.7	9	37	12	8.9 %	12.4 %	11.0 %
ISO certification	–	5	24	8	5.0 %	8.0 %	7.3 %
Support system selection	–	4	16	6	4.0 %	5.4 %	5.5 %
Total		101	299	109	100.0 %	100.0 %	100.0 %

Table 4-31: Reasons to describe processes per department ($N_{IT} = 88$; $N_{BPM} = 38$; $N_{CO} = 22$; $N_{FA} = 16$) – Q5

Answers	Count (c_i)				Percentage ($c_i / \Sigma c_i$)			
	IT	BPM	CO	FA	IT	BPM	CO	FA
Business process reengineering	65	33	15	10	17.6 %	20.0 %	17.4 %	20.8 %
Documentation	54	25	13	9	14.6 %	15.2 %	15.1 %	18.8 %
Automate process execution	54	24	8	6	14.6 %	14.5 %	9.3 %	12.5 %
Integration of software systems	44	19	9	3	11.9 %	11.5 %	10.5 %	6.3 %
Guidelines	63	28	19	9	17.1 %	17.0 %	22.1 %	18.8 %
Monitoring process execution	41	19	14	4	11.1 %	11.5 %	16.3 %	8.3 %
ISO certification	28	11	4	3	7.6 %	6.7 %	4.7 %	6.3 %
Support system selection	20	6	4	4	5.4 %	3.6 %	4.7 %	8.3 %
Total	369	165	86	48	100.0 %	100.0 %	100.0 %	100.0 %

Process descriptions in non-BPM software (Q6): All the reasons for process descriptions mentioned so far are derived from the BPM life cycle (see Section 3.1). However, process descriptions are also created as part of non-BPM software; see Table 4-32. Most companies of each region stated that they model processes in order to use general software such as ERP systems and similar (e.g. CRM, SCM, procurement or HR systems), integration software and data warehouses. These software types are not isolated from BPM because they are involved in the execution of business processes, see question (Q18), Table 4-10, in Section 4.2. The regional differences concerning the software types (answer category 'yes') are not significant ($\chi^2_{ma} = 6.11$; df = 8; p = 0.635).

Table 4-32: Process models in non-BPM software per region ($N_{NA} = 26$; $N_{EU} = 72$; $N_O = 26$) – Q6

Answers	ML	Count (c_i)			Percentage ($c_i / \Sigma c_i$)		
		NA	EU	O	NA	EU	O
Yes	–	15	27	15	30.0 %	21.6 %	25.9 %
No		8	33	8	16.0 %	26.4 %	13.8 %
ERP systems and similar	4	11	21	15	22.0 %	16.8 %	25.9 %
Integration software	3	8	20	11	16.0 %	16.0 %	19.0 %
Data warehouse	3	6	13	6	12.0 %	10.4 %	10.3 %
Requirement engineering software	–	2	11	3	4.0 %	8.8 %	5.2 %
Total		50	125	58	100.0 %	100.0 %	100.0 %

Process description styles (Q4): The specific reasons for process descriptions require distinct process description styles. The dominant process description style in each region is text, see Table 4-33. Process modelling with various kinds of languages is more common in Europe (45.6 % in total) than in North America (38 % in total) or the 'other' countries (21.3 % in total). Among the process modelling languages, the BPMN [OMG11] prevails in Europe; it is as prominent as the UML [OMG10] and the Integrated Definition IDEF [NIST93] are in North America and is widely outperformed by the UML in the 'other' countries. The even-driven process chain (EPC) [ScTA05] is mainly used by European companies. In each region, as indicated by the total of counts, some companies use more than one process description style; five European companies and one from another country even use several process modelling languages. Because of the low cell counts in Table 4-33, the modified Pearson chi-square test cannot be applied to check the significance of language usage, but the regions differ significantly at the level of the aggregated answers 'as text', 'as tables', and 'with languages' (χ^2_{ma} = 16.37; df = 6; p = 0.012). As open answers to question (Q4), mainly flowcharts as well as proprietary languages of tools were mentioned.

Table 4-33: Current documentation of processes per region (N_{NA} = 22; N_{EU} = 63; N_O = 27) – Q4 **

Answers	ML	Count (c_i)			Percentage ($c_i / \Sigma c_i$)		
		NA	EU	O	NA	EU	O
As text	2	15	36	20	35.7 %	35.0 %	42.6 %
As tables	2+	7	19	14	16.7 %	18.4 %	29.8 %
With languages	BPMN	4	20	1	9.5 %	19.4 %	2.1 %
	UML	4	10	5	9.5 %	9.7 %	10.6 %
	EPC	3	11	2	7.1 %	10.7 %	4.3 %
	BPEL	2	2	2	2.4 %	1.9 %	4.3 %
	IDEF	0	4	0	9.5 %	3.9 %	0.0 %
Other		4	1	3	9.6 %	1.0 %	6.3 %
Total		38	103	47	100.0 %	100.0 %	100.0 %

Note: ML column values for With languages rows = 2.7

Table 4-34: Current documentation of processes per department (N_{IT} = 77; N_{BPM} = 32; N_{CO} = 19; N_{FA} = 14) – Q4**

Answers		Count (c_i)				Percentage ($c_i / \Sigma c_i$)			
		IT	BPM	CO	FA	IT	BPM	CO	FA
As text		51	16	9	11	37.2 %	30.8 %	29.0 %	45.8 %
As tables		31	8	6	6	22.6 %	15.4 %	19.4 %	25.0 %
With languages	BPMN	13	13	10	2	9.5 %	25.0 %	32.3 %	8.3 %
	UML	16	3	3	2	11.8 %	5.8 %	9.7 %	8.3 %
	EPC	13	7	2	2	9.5 %	13.5 %	6.5 %	8.3 %
	BPEL	5	1	0	0	3.6 %	1.9 %	0.0 %	0.0 %
	IDEF	3	2	0	0	2.2 %	3.8 %	0.0 %	0.0 %
Other		5	2	1	1	3.6 %	3.8 %	3.1 %	4.3 %
Total		137	52	31	24	100.0 %	100.0 %	100.0 %	100.0 %

Table 4-34 shows the answers to question (Q4) per department of the representative who filled in the questionnaire. In most departments, text is the preferred process description style, followed by tables and some kind of process modelling. Most process modelling occurs in BPM departments (50 % in total), followed by departments for company organization (48.5 % in total) and IT (36.6 % in total), whereas process modelling is rather unpopular in functional areas (24.9 % in total). Departments for company organization especially favour the BPMN, in BPM departments the BPMN is still more widespread than the EPC. At the aggregated level (answers 'as text', 'as tables', and 'with languages'), the differences between the departments are significant (χ^2_{ma} = 23.03; df = 12; p = 0.028), though the results of the modified Pearson chi-square may be affected by the unbalanced cell counts.

Since the way in which process descriptions are created might well influence the modelling requirements, the companies were asked about the organization (Q3) and procedure (Q16) of process documentation.

Organization of process modelling (Q3): In all regions, process descriptions are mostly created within the departments and then centrally aligned, see Table 4-35. Process documentation by a central BPM team is most common in Europe, whereas North American companies also totally decentralize process documentation; see Table 5. However, the regional differences just miss significance at the α = 0.1 level (χ^2_{ma} = 9.85; df = 6; p = 0.143).

Table 4-35: Company-internal organization of process design (N_{NA} = 26; N_{EU} = 74; N_O = 29) – Q3

Answers	ML	Count (c_i)			Percentage ($c_i / \Sigma c_i$)		
		NA	EU	O	NA	EU	O
Within departments, then centrally aligned	2.5	15	43	14	42.9 %	42.6 %	42.4 %
Within departments without alignment	2	15	27	10	42.9 %	26.7 %	30.3 %
By central BPM team	2.5	5	31	9	14.3 %	30.7 %	27.3 %
Total		35	101	33	100.0 %	100.0 %	100.0 %

Irrespective of the companies' regions, process design mostly *starts (Q16) from* the interactions between participants, followed by goals and activities of the business processes, see Table 4-36. A product and its transformation from an initial to a final form is the second most important starting point for process design in North American companies and BPM departments, but comes last in all other regions and departments. In contrast to IT and BPM departments, departments for company organization and functional areas prefer the goals and activities of a process as a starting point for process modelling, see Table 4-37. The differences between the regions (χ^2_{ma} = 8.49; df = 6; p = 0.205) and departments (χ^2_{ma} = 10.32; df = 12; p = 0.588) are not significant.

Table 4-36: Procedure for process design per region - Q16

Answers	Count (c_i)			Percentage ($c_i / \Sigma c_i$)		
	NA	EU	O	NA	EU	O
Product	11	25	8	29.7 %	26.3 %	19.5 %
Goals and activities	8	35	14	21.6 %	36.8 %	34.1 %
Interactions	18	35	19	48.6 %	36.8 %	46.3 %
Total	37	95	41	100.0 %	100.0 %	100.0 %

Table 4-37: Procedure for process design per department - Q16

Answers	Count (c_i)				Percentage ($c_i / \Sigma c_i$)			
	IT	BPM	CO	FA	IT	BPM	CO	FA
Product	29	17	9	9	25.4 %	32.1 %	26.5 %	26.5 %
Goals and activities	36	15	13	13	31.6 %	28.3 %	38.2 %	38.2 %
Interactions	49	21	12	12	43.0 %	39.6 %	35.3 %	35.3 %
Total	114	53	34	34	100.0 %	100.0 %	100.0 %	100.0 %

Basic process modelling concepts (Q19): The counts in Table 4-33 indicate that many companies complement textual descriptions with process models. Process automation as another reason to document processes (see Table 4-30) also demands more precision than can be achieved with text in a natural language. Thus there is a need for process modelling languages, and we asked the companies which concepts they need in these languages to describe their business processes (Q19). The most important concepts were examined more closely by the additional questions (Q20) to (Q24).

According to the mean ratings, tasks to be done in the process (*activities*) are by far the most important concept for process descriptions, followed by relationships, persons or roles, documents and resources, see Table

4-38. Time information and timely distances between tasks are rated as least important. When asked openly to list other concepts needed, constructs to describe exceptions and exception handling were mentioned most often, immediately followed by business rules and the data flow between tasks. Here, the companies did not recognize that exceptions are a special type of event, which come second last in Table 4-38. The regional variations concerning the concepts needed are not significant.

Table 4-38: Basic concepts in process models per region ($N_{NA} = 26$; $N_{EU} = 75$; $N_O = 29$) - Q19

Answer (Rating scale type 1)	μ			σ			Rank		
	NA	EU	O	NA	EU	O	NA	EU	O
Tasks to be done in process (*activities*)	1.38	1.29	1.41	0.50	0.63	0.73	1	1	1
Relationships between tasks	1.54	1.59	1.69	0.58	0.92	0.85	2	2	2
Persons or roles who execute the tasks	1.73	1.63	1.72	0.72	0.91	0.80	3	3	3
Documents or objects resulting from a task	1.81	1.93	2.00	0.80	0.86	0.89	4	4	4
Resources needed to fulfil the tasks	2.19	2.23	2.17	0.80	0.88	1.00	5	6	5
Time information related to task	2.35	2.51	2.28	0.75	0.99	0.70	6	7	6
Events that happen and influence a task	2.35	2.21	2.28	0.80	0.87	0.88	7	5	7
Timely distances between end & start of task	2.58	2.69	2.69	0.90	1.00	0.76	8	8	8

Table 4-40 analyzes the answers to question (Q19) per department. Again, tasks to be done in the process are the most important concept. Now, however, the persons or roles executing the tasks come second in all departments – except for the IT department. For the IT department, the relationships between the tasks take the second place, yet rank third in most other departments. Altogether the variation between the departments concerning the importance of the concepts is not significant.

Nature of relationships (Q20): After tasks, the second most important concept in all regions are relationships (see Table 4-38). In question (Q20) the participants had to assess the frequency of distinct types of relationships. Fairly obviously, sequences are the most common type of relationships, followed by split and merge, see Table 4-39. Loops and alternative tasks (XOR-splits) are rare. Conditions can apply to various kinds of relationship; these are investigated in more detail in question (Q21A). The listed order of relationship types applies to all regions (see Table 4-39) and all departments (see Table 4-41); the observable differences are not significant.

Table 4-39: Task relationships per region ($N_{NA} = 26$; $N_{EU} = 75$; $N_O = 29$) - Q20

Answer (Rating scale type 2)	μ			σ			Rank		
	NA	EU	O	NA	EU	O	NA	EU	O
Tasks follow strict sequence	2.42	2.27	2.28	0.70	0.64	0.84	1	1	2
Condition must be satisfied in order to start a task	2.50	2.40	2.38	0.51	0.57	0.78	2	2	4
Task has more than one immediate successor (split)	2.50	2.55	2.24	0.76	0.58	0.74	2	3	1
Task has more than one immediate predecessor (merge)	2.62	2.65	2.34	0.57	0.63	0.72	3	4	3
Task is repeated till some criterion is satisfied (looping)	2.77	2.92	2.59	0.71	0.77	0.83	4	5	5
Tasks are alternative to each other	3.19	3.25	2.90	0.85	0.74	0.94	5	6	6

Splits (Q21), which are the third most important relationship type (see Table 4-39), represent the situation in which a task has several successors. Table 4-42 and Table 4-43 summarize per region and per department, respectively, the companies' answers about what happens with the successors. Mostly, all of the successors are executed (AND split), either concurrently (with synchronization) or independently of each other (without synchronization). If not all succeeding tasks are executed (OR split), the selection mostly depends on a condition (see Question (Q21A) for the nature of conditions). In line with the results of Question (Q20), exclusive choices

Table 4-40: Basic concepts in process models per department ($N_{IT} = 88$; $N_{BPM} = 38$; $N_{CO} = 22$; $N_{FA} = 16$) - Q19

Answer (Rating scale type 1)	μ				σ				Rank			
	IT	BPM	CO	FA	IT	BPM	CO	FA	IT	BPM	CO	FA
Tasks to be done in process (activities)	1.39	1.34	1.18	1.31	0.65	0.71	0.40	0.60	1	1	1	1
Relationships between tasks	1.63	1.58	1.86	1.75	0.81	1.06	1.04	1.13	2	2	3	3
Persons or roles who execute the tasks	1.75	1.58	1.45	1.50	0.91	0.89	0.60	0.73	3	2	2	2
Documents or objects resulting from a task	1.89	1.84	2.05	2.00	0.86	0.68	0.90	0.82	4	3	4	4
Resources needed to fulfil the tasks	2.11	2.13	2.45	2.69	0.81	0.94	0.91	0.79	5	4	7	7
Time information related to task	2.26	2.24	2.14	2.19	0.88	0.82	0.77	0.83	6	5	5	5
Events that happen and influence a task	2.45	2.37	2.27	2.25	0.91	0.79	0.88	0.78	7	6	6	6
Timely distances between end & start of task	2.82	3.00	2.95	2.88	0.92	0.93	0.84	1.03	8	7	8	8

Table 4-41: Task relationships per department ($N_{IT} = 88$; $N_{BPM} = 38$; $N_{CO} = 22$; $N_{FA} = 16$) - Q20

Answer (Rating scale type 2)	μ				σ				Rank			
	IT	BPM	CO	FA	IT	BPM	CO	FA	IT	BPM	CO	FA
Tasks follow strict sequence	2.31	2.26	2.18	2.31	0.75	0.72	0.59	0.70	1	1	1	1
Condition must be satisfied in order to start a task	2.39	2.47	2.36	2.50	0.65	0.69	0.58	0.73	2	2	2	2
Task has more than one immediate successor (split)	2.42	2.55	2.55	2.50	0.62	0.65	0.60	0.63	3	3	3	2
Task has more than one immediate predecessor (merge)	2.51	2.66	2.73	2.56	0.63	0.67	0.70	0.73	4	4	4	3
Task is repeated till some criterion is satisfied (looping)	2.83	2.87	2.73	2.75	0.82	0.88	0.70	0.86	5	5	4	4
Tasks are alternative to each other	3.09	3.21	3.14	3.25	0.78	0.94	0.83	0.93	6	6	5	5

Table 4-42: Execution of succeeding tasks per region - Q21

Answer (Rating scale type 2)	N/na				μ				σ				Rank			
	NA	EU	O	FA	NA	EU	O		NA	EU	O		NA	EU	O	
All and concurrently (AND)	25/1	60/15	23/6		2.64	2.67	2.57		0.70	0.73	0.90		1	1	1	
All, independent of each other (AND)	23/3	64/11	22/7		3.09	2.94	2.95		0.67	0.69	0.79		2	2	3	
Not all tasks are executed (OR)	23/3	61/14	22/7		3.26	3.36	2.91		0.69	0.90	0.81		3	3	2	
Which tasks are executed depends on…																
…random selection	20/6	57/18	22/7		4.10	4.25	3.68		0.72	0.74	1.17		3-IV	3-IV	2-IV	
…some selection condition is satisfied	23/3	62/13	22/7		2.70	2.55	2.41		0.70	0.78	0.59		3-I	3-I	2-I	
…subjective experience	23/3	60/15	23/6		3.22	3.30	3.00		0.74	0.83	0.85		3-II	3-II	2-II	
As soon as one task has been executed, no other task is performed (XOR)	21/5	55/20	22/7		3.29	3.33	3.18		0.85	0.86	1.14		3-III	3-III	2-III	

Table 4-43: Execution of succeeding tasks per department - Q21

Answer (Rating scale type 2)	N/na				μ				σ				Rank			
	IT	BPM	CO	FA	IT	BPM	CO	FA	IT	BPM	CO	FA	IT	BPM	CO	FA
All and concurrently (AND)	76/12	32/6	16/6	14/2	2.70	2.88	2.38	2.36	0.75	0.83	0.72	0.75	1	1	1	1
All, independent of each other (AND)	75/13	32/6	15/7	14/2	3.04	3.16	2.60	2.93	0.67	0.72	0.74	0.92	2	2	2	2
Not all tasks are executed (OR)	74/14	30/8	14/8	12/4	3.15	3.43	3.14	3.42	0.81	1.00	0.77	1.08	3	3	3	3
Which tasks are executed depends on…																
…random selection	69/19	32/6	11/11	11/5	3.99	4.28	4.09	4.36	0.87	0.73	0.94	1.03	3-IV	3-IV	3-IV	3-IV
…some selection condition is satisfied	73/15	31/7	15/7	13/3	2.47	2.45	2.73	2.92	0.69	0.77	0.70	0.76	3-I	3-I	3-I	3-I
…subjective experience	73/15	32/6	14/8	13/3	3.14	3.50	3.14	3.31	0.77	0.92	0.86	0.75	3-II	3-III	3-III	3-II
As soon as one task has been executed, no other task is performed (XOR)	71/17	27/11	11/11	11/5	3.23	3.19	3.00	3.82	0.87	1.04	1.00	0.98	3-III	3-II	3-II	3-III

(XOR splits) are not very frequent. This assessment of splits applies to companies from each region and to all departments; the minor differences are not statistically significant.

Nature of conditions (Q21A): Conditions are the second most important relationship type as they start tasks in sequences or guide the selection of tasks in OR/XOR splits. Question (Q21A) investigated the nature of conditions in more detail, see Table 4-44. In European companies and companies from the 'other' countries, conditions mostly refer to the results of adjacent tasks, whereas in North American companies the majority of conditions refer to the overall state of the process. In third position are conditions that depend on the task only, e.g. the availability of resources. Information external to the process plays a (subordinate) role for European and North American companies, and in both regions time information (e.g., start times, intervals, and durations) is the least important condition type. For companies from the 'other' countries, the order of the last two ranks is interchanged, see Table 4-44.

Table 4-44: Nature of conditions per region – Q21A

Answers	ML	Count (c_i)			Percentage ($c_i / \Sigma c_i$)		
		NA	EU	O	NA	EU	O
The tasks only		14	42	14	18.9 %	20.6 %	18.4 %
The results of adjacent tasks		18	53	21	24.3 %	26.0 %	27.6 %
The overall state of the process		20	44	18	27.0 %	21.6 %	23.7 %
Information external to the process		13	37	10	17.6 %	18.1 %	13.2 %
Time		9	28	13	12.2 %	13.7 %	17.1 %
Total		74	204	76	100.0 %	100.0 %	100.0 %

The evaluation of the answers to Question (Q21A) per department (see Table 4-45) makes even more clear that the results of adjacent tasks constitute the most important source for conditions, followed by the overall process state. Neither the differences among the regions ($\chi^2_{ma} = 6.09$; df = 10; p = 0.807) nor the differences among the departments are significant ($\chi^2_{ma} = 19.09$; df = 20; p = 0.518).

Table 4-45: Nature of conditions per department – Q21A

Answers	Count (c_i)				Percentage ($c_i / \Sigma c_i$)			
	IT	BPM	CO	FA	IT	BPM	CO	FA
The tasks only	37	4	5	7	21.8 %	12.5 %	20.0 %	20.0 %
The results of adjacent tasks	42	10	8	9	24.7 %	31.3 %	32.0 %	25.7 %
The overall state of the process	41	8	4	8	24.1 %	25.0 %	16.0 %	22.9 %
Information external to the process	28	5	4	6	16.5 %	15.6 %	16.0 %	17.1 %
Time	22	5	4	5	12.9 %	15.6 %	16.0 %	14.3 %
Total	170	32	25	35	100.0 %	100.0 %	100.0 %	100.0 %

Information about persons (Q23): For the departments (see Table 4-40), information about persons or roles was the second most important concept for process descriptions. Across all regions (see Table 4-47) and departments (see Table 4-46), the capabilities needed to execute a task are the most important information companies want to express about roles, followed by organizational units and names. The differences among the regions ($\chi^2_{ma} = 12.44$; df = 8; p = 0.133) and departments ($\chi^2_{ma} = 19.57$; df = 16; p = 0.240) are not significant; however, the low cell counts affect the validity of the modified Pearson chi-square test.

Table 4-46: Required information about persons per region – Q23

Answers	Count (c_i)			Percentage ($c_i / \Sigma c_i$)		
	NA	EU	O	NA	EU	O
None	0	2	3	0.0 %	1.4 %	4.8 %
Required capabilities	24	64	22	46.2 %	45.4 %	35.5 %
Names of responsible persons	9	22	15	17.3 %	15.6 %	24.2 %
Organizational units	19	53	22	36.5 %	37.6 %	35.5 %
Total	52	141	62	100.0 %	100.0 %	100.0 %

Table 4-47: Required information about persons per department – Q23

Answers	Count (c_i)				Percentage ($c_i / \Sigma c_i$)			
	IT	BPM	CO	FA	IT	BPM	CO	FA
None	2	1	0	0	1.6 %	4.3 %	0.0 %	0.0 %
Required capabilities	53	11	12	8	43.1 %	47.8 %	44.4 %	57.1 %
Names of responsible persons	24	3	5	2	19.5 %	13.0 %	18.5 %	14.3 %
Organizational units	44	8	10	4	35.8 %	34.8 %	37.0 %	28.6 %
Total	123	23	27	14	100.0 %	100.0 %	100.0 %	100.0 %

Resources in processes (Q22): Table 4-48 and Table 4-49 show, per region and per department, which resources companies need in order to describe processes. Mostly, information is the most needed resource, followed by documents and personnel. Note that 'information' (immaterial) and 'document' (material) do not necessarily coincide. In companies from the 'other' countries, personnel and information are equally important, and software systems share the second rank with documents (see Table 4-48). The blurred distinction between information and documents becomes visible from the very similar ranking of these answer alternatives in Table 4-49. Overall, machines and appliances are the resource least required for process descriptions – even in functional areas (see Table 4-49). The differences in the regional ratings of machines and appliances (H = 8.69; df = 2; p = 0.013) and material (H = 11.47; df = 2; p = 0.003) are significant. Among the departments, only the different rating of 'documents' as a resource is significant (H = 10.86; df = 4; p = 0.028).

Table 4-48: Resources needed in process models per region (N_{NA} = 26; N_{EU} = 75; N_O = 29) - Q22(**)

Answer (Rating scale type 1)	µ			σ			Rank		
	NA	EU	O	NA	EU	O	NA	EU	O
Information	1.58	1.48	1.62	0.64	0.60	0.62	1	1	1
Documents	1.88	1.68	1.90	0.65	0.68	0.77	2	2	2
Personnel	1.88	1.69	1.62	0.82	0.87	0.86	2	3	1
Software systems	1.92	2.03	1.90	0.85	1.03	0.86	3	4	2
Material**	2.38	3.03	2.34	0.70	1.19	1.01	4	5	3
Machines, appliances**	2.88	3.27	2.59	0.95	1.17	1.05	5	6	4

Additional concepts for processes (Q24): The Questions (Q19) to (Q23) dealt with constructs provided by most process modelling languages. We also wanted to know whether the companies need *additional concepts* to describe their processes or tasks. As it can be seen in Table 4-50 and Table 4-51 the execution status (started, cancelled, etc.) is the concept most needed for describing *tasks*, followed by priorities, whereas goals (see Table 4-51) and cost (see Table 4-50) are mainly required to describe *processes*. The planning status seems to be relevant only in functional areas, whereas departments for company organization particularly want to include cost information in their descriptions. The regionally differing ratings for the planning status (for process: H = 6.38; df = 2; p = 0.041; for task: H = 5.51; df = 2; p = 0.064) and the task execution status (H = 7.83; df = 2; p = 0.020) are significant.

Table 4-49: Resources needed in process models per department ($N_{IT} = 88$; $N_{BPM} = 38$; $N_{CO} = 22$; $N_{FA} = 16$) - Q22(**)

Answer (Rating scale type 1)	μ				σ				Rank			
	IT	BPM	CO	FA	IT	BPM	CO	FA	IT	BPM	CO	FA
Information	1.55	1.42	1.59	1.81	0.62	0.60	0.66	0.75	1	1	1	2
Documents**	1.73	1.58	1.59	1.75	0.80	0.95	0.66	0.78	2	3	1	1
Personnel	1.81	1.50	1.86	1.81	0.66	0.65	0.77	0.83	3	2	2	2
Software systems	1.92	1.82	2.00	2.06	0.91	1.01	0.98	0.68	4	4	3	3
Material	2.73	3.03	2.95	2.69	1.08	1.26	1.17	1.01	5	5	4	4
Machines, appliances	2.95	3.21	3.14	3.19	1.08	1.12	1.25	1.22	6	6	5	5

Table 4-50: Additional concepts needed in process models ($N_{IT} = 63$; $N_{BPM} = 30$; $N_{CO} = 17$; $N_{FA} = 9$) - Q24

Department	Answer (Special rating scale)	Execution status		Priorities		Goals		Cost		Planning status	
		Task	Process	Task	Process	Task	Process	Task	Process	Task	Process
IT Department	Needed (c_i)	48	43	43	38	35	39	34	52	28	36
	Percentage ($c_i/\sum c_i$)	(26 %)	(21 %)	(23 %)	(18 %)	(19 %)	(19 %)	(18 %)	(25 %)	(15 %)	(17 %)
BPM Department	Needed (c_i)	24	22	18	18	12	20	16	27	10	12
	Percentage ($c_i/\sum c_i$)	(30 %)	(22 %)	(23 %)	(18 %)	(15 %)	(20 %)	(20 %)	(27 %)	(13 %)	(12 %)
CO Department	Needed (c_i)	7	11	8	8	8	9	12	15	5	7
	Percentage ($c_i/\sum c_i$)	(18 %)	(22 %)	(20 %)	(16 %)	(20 %)	(18 %)	(30 %)	(30 %)	(13 %)	(14 %)
FA Department	Needed (c_i)	9	7	4	5	5	11	3	6	7	8
	Percentage ($c_i/\sum c_i$)	(32 %)	(19 %)	(14 %)	(14 %)	(17 %)	(30 %)	(11 %)	(16 %)	(25 %)	(22 %)

Table 4-51: Additional concepts needed in process models ($N_{NA} = 23$; $N_{EU} = 56$; $N_O = 16$) - Q24 (**)

Region	Answer (Special rating scale)	Execution status		Priorities		Goals		Cost		Planning status**	
		Task**	Process	Task	Process	Task	Process	Task	Process	Task	Process
North America	Needed (c_i)	20	16	18	14	14	15	11	16	14	15
	Percentage ($c_i/\sum c_i$)	(26 %)	(21 %)	(23 %)	(18 %)	(18 %)	(20 %)	(14 %)	(21 %)	(18 %)	(20 %)
Europe	Needed (c_i)	38	40	31	32	31	48	28	34	20	29
	Percentage ($c_i/\sum c_i$)	(26 %)	(22 %)	(21 %)	(18 %)	(21 %)	(26 %)	(19 %)	(19 %)	(14 %)	(16 %)
Other	Needed (c_i)	13	12	12	8	9	17	9	8	10	12
	Percentage ($c_i/\sum c_i$)	(25 %)	(25 %)	(23 %)	(14 %)	(17 %)	(35 %)	(17 %)	(16 %)	(19 %)	(25 %)

5 Interpretation of the Empirical Results

5.1 Discussion of the Findings

In the following we summarize the gathered results, connect them with each other, draw conclusions and compare our results with other empirical investigations. In addition to short descriptions of our findings, Table 5-1 shows the questions from which they were directly or indirectly derived, their statistical significance at the $\alpha = 0.05$ (**) or $\alpha = 0.1$ (*) level respectively, as well as similar findings that have been reported in the relevant literature.

Nature of processes (see Section 4.2): Current business processes are to a limited extent inter-organizational as they span on average four departments in a company and involve only one to two other organizations (Q34), (Q33). This observation is indirectly supported by the fact that software for supply chain management (SCM) and applications at business partners are not among the top five software application used in business processes; instead, ERP systems prevail (Q18). A decline in the popularity of SCM software from 20 % in 2004 to 12 % in 2006 was also detected by the study "Status Quo of BPM" [Neub09].

The processes are equally triggered by information sent from business partners and company-internal information (Q17), which matches the above described distribution of processes (four departments and one to two business partners; see Question (Q34)). The third most important process trigger is timing; this is in line with the process scope (Q15).

Most processes deal with products/services of a company or its customers (e.g. order management, claims handling) as well as software (development and project management, systems integration, change management) (Q15), (Q13). As opposed to software, products and customers are well-known, historical objects of BPM [PrAr99], [WoHa10], [SmMM09]. Consistently with this *process scope*, timing, increased customer satisfaction and quality are the most important process *goals* (Q25).

Timing is generally crucial for business processes as these are quite short-term, especially in Europe and in the 'other' countries, where most business processes have a run time that is measured in days and are executed several times a day ((Q35), (Q36)). Long-running processes, which are measured in weeks or months, mainly occur in North American companies.

In spite of the short execution time horizon, business processes are quite *stable*. They are changed yearly or rarely (Q27) to keep up with the evolving business or as a reaction to influences from the environment (Q30), and the changes tend to be minor (Q28). In most cases the changes apply to all future executions of the business process; ad-hoc changes for just the current process execution mainly occur in functional areas (Q29).

Software for BPM (see Section 4.3): Process design, enactment and monitoring are the major BPM phases to be supported by software. The following results can be consistently generalized from the answers to the Questions (Q18) and (Q11).

An average business process involves four software applications (Q34). The most common application types in *process execution* (Q18) are databases/data ware houses, ERP systems and office software. CRM systems rank fourth, which supports 'customer contact' and 'order management' as scopes of processes (Q15). The substantial contribution of ERP and CRM systems to process execution is confirmed by the study "Status Quo of BPM" [Neub09], where, however, proprietary systems rank second in the order of applications that support process execution.

In order to *design* their *processes* (Q11) most companies currently prefer simple drawing tools such as Microsoft Visio, office software (such as Microsoft Word), ERP systems (especially the ones from SAP, which contain a workflow component) and in-house solutions. The dominance of Microsoft Visio (and Powerpoint) for process modelling is known (see [Reck08], [WoHa10]), but only a minority of the companies surveyed in these investigations use in-house solutions.

BPM systems and suites currently play a negligible role during process execution (Q18) and design (Q11). The comparatively low prevalence of BPM suites was also noted by other investigations [Neub09], [WoHa10]. Our results show that mainly two BPM suites could prevail (Q11): IBM Websphere BPM, which is globally used, and the ARIS toolset, which is especially prominent in European companies and in BPM departments. Both BPM suites are treated differently elsewhere. According to [WoHa10], IBM Websphere is the dominating

BPM suite, while the ARIS toolset is not mentioned at all in this investigation; the reverse situation occurs in [Reck08].

The companies *selected* the *applications* they use for process description and management mainly because of their functionalities and qualities, followed by pricing and support (Q12). North-American companies as well as IT and BPM departments are especially price-conscious, whereas support is more crucial for the other regions and departments.

Thus software for BPM is selected because it satisfies distinct *requirements* (Q8). The most important requirement of the companies is usability, i.e. obvious, easy-to-learn and efficient human-computer interaction. Usability is largely followed by modelling capabilities, report generation, software integration and alignment to standards. Departments for IT, BPM and company organization in particular emphasize report generation, whereas in functional areas software integration and process monitoring are more appreciated capabilities. The fact that software integration ranks comparatively highly is consistent with the use of about four applications in an average business process, as well as with the involvement of one to two business partners (Q34). Altogether the integration requirements directly follow from the reasons for describing processes (Q5) and the process scope (Q15).

The necessity of *modelling capabilities* is empirically confirmed [Neub09], [Reck08] and is accompanied by requirements for model publication, model repositories, navigations between models and adaptability. The functionalities of process simulation, monitoring and controlling are also mentioned occasionally [Neub09]. In projects that implemented BPM software in a company's organization, process monitoring turned out to be especially useful because it helped in identifying the poor parts of a process [KüHa07]. Moreover, these projects also made clear that software integration capabilities are needed [KüHa07], which agrees with our results, but is usually neglected in the context of BPM.

Automated *process execution* is not urgently required by the companies – it ranks third to sixth; the higher ratings apply to European companies, departments for company organization and functional areas (Q8). Other investigations even see model-driven process execution as a major challenge of BPM [InRR09b].

During process execution most companies want software to execute tasks, to route tasks or to provide information; totally automated process execution is not a necessity (Q9). This result is consistent with the use of software during process execution (Q18). For example ERP, CRM or procurement systems that are used in most business processes merely execute tasks; office software, which also includes e-mail programs, can route tasks, and databases or data warehouses – the most frequent software applications in business processes – provide information. The low appreciation of automated process execution is in line with the low dissemination of BPM suites (Q18). However, the companies that model their processes with the BPMN seem to attach importance to process automation [Reck08].

Process monitoring is the third most important requirement for BPM software in functional areas (Q8) and the third most important reason to describe business processes for organization departments (Q5). In particular, the task/process status, times and failures in process execution are to be monitored (Q10). All of this information is closely related to customer contact and satisfaction as process scope (Q15) and goal (Q25). Furthermore, this kind of monitoring supports the timing goals of business processes (Q25).

Describing processes (see Section 4.4): Describing processes is a fundamental part of process design – and is also important beyond the intentions of BPM. The main *reasons* for describing processes are (in order of decreasing importance): preparing business process reengineering, documenting 'as-is' processes, having guidelines for persons executing the processes, automating process execution and software integration (Q5). The latter two reasons are *software-centric*, all other ones *human-centric*. The software-centric reasons correlate with the fact that process descriptions are also contained in ERP systems, integration software and data warehouses (Q6). As these software types are used in the execution of business processes (Q18), there is no strict line between BPM reasons and non-BPM reasons for describing processes.

When inquiring with BPM experts regarding the perceived benefits of process modelling, similar human-centric reasons (process improvement, understanding, and communication) were mentioned [InRR09a]. Moreover, process documentation, analysis and improvement have been found to be the main purposes for modelling processes with the BPMN [Reck08]. This, on the whole, also confirms our results.

The purpose of creating process descriptions determines the *process description* style. Most companies document their business processes as text or tables (Q4). These description styles perfectly support the human-centric purposes of describing processes, which are pursued more intensively by the companies than the soft-

Table 5-1: Summary of the findings

Finding	Supported by question(s) Directly	Supported by question(s) Indirectly	Significance	Other investigations
Nature of business processes				
Mainly internal, 1-2 business partners	(Q34), (Q33)	(Q18), (Q17)	—	[Neub09]
Scope				
Products/services, Customer	(Q15), (Q13)	(Q25) (Q17) Timing (Q18) CRM systems	**	[WoHa10]: reduce costs, improve productivity and flexibility, customer satisfaction; [PrAr99], [SmMM09]
Software				—
Short-term: run time and execution frequency measured in days	(Q35), (Q36)	(Q17) Timing	(**)	—
Stable: i.e. rare and minor changes for all future executions in line with the evolving business and reactive to environment	(Q27) to (Q30)	—	(**)	—
Software for BPM				
Process design				
Drawing tools (Microsoft Visio), office software (Microsoft Word), ERP systems, in-house solutions	(Q11)	(Q15), (Q18)	**	[Reck08], [WoHa10]: Microsoft Visio, Powerpoint
Process enactment				
On average 4 applications involved	(Q34)		—	—
Mainly databases, ERP systems, office software, CRM systems	(Q18)	(Q11)	—	[Neub09]: ERP, CRM, proprietary systems
Process automation not urgently required	(Q8)	(Q5)	(**)	[InRR09b]: Major challenge
Software should execute tasks, route tasks or provide information	(Q9)	(Q18)	—	—
Process monitoring				
3rd most important software functionality	(Q8)	(Q5)	—	[KüHa07]
Mainly status, times, failures	(Q10)	(Q15), (Q25)	—	—
BPM tools/systems/suites				
Overall negligible	(Q18), (Q11)	—	**	[Neub09], [WoHa10]
Mainly IBM Websphere (worldwide) and ARIS toolset (Europe)	(Q11)	—	**	[WoHa10]: IBM Websphere [Reck08]: ARIS
Selected because of functionalities/qualities, pricing, support	(Q12)	(Q8) in relation with (Q11)	**	—
Most important requirements: Usability, modelling capabilities, report generation, software integration	(Q8)	(Q11), (Q34), (Q5), (Q15)	(**)	[Neub09], [Reck08]: process modelling [KüHa07]: software integration, process monitoring
Process description				
Reasons: mainly human-centric (prepare business process reengineering, documentation, guidelines), a few software-centric (process automation, integration)	(Q5)	(Q6), (Q18)	**	[InRR09a]: process improvement, understanding, communication [Reck08]: process documentation, improvement, analysis
Style: Mainly text, complemented with process models	(Q4)	(Q5), (Q11)	**	—
Process modelling				
More common in Europe and in BPM/CO departments than elsewhere	(Q4)	—	**	[WoHa10]: Europe
Mainly with the BPMN, followed by UML activity diagrams and EPC	(Q4)	(Q11)	—	[WoHa10], but without EPC
EPC mainly in Europe & BPM departments	(Q4)	(Q11)	—	—
Most important *concepts*: task, relationships, persons/roles, documents, resources	(Q19)	(Q22)	—	[zMRI08] for the BPMN: task, sequence flow, start/end event, pool, general/ parallel gateway
Task looping and XOR-splits not common	(Q20)	(Q21)	—	[zMRI08]
Conditions mostly refer to adjacent tasks or overall process state	(Q21A)	—	—	—
Most important *resources*: information, documents, personnel, software	(Q22)	(Q19)	(**)	—
About personnel mainly capabilities and organizational units	(Q23)	(Q5)	(**)	—
Additionally: execution status, goals, cost	(Q24)	(Q25), (Q5)	(**)	—

ware-centric purposes (Q5). In addition to textual descriptions the majority of companies use process modelling (Q4). Altogether, these description styles coincide with the software used to describe and manage processes (Q11) since the dominating BPM tools Microsoft Word and Microsoft Visio facilitate process descriptions by text and with (various) process modelling languages.

Process modelling seems to be more common in Europe as well as in departments for BPM or company organization than elsewhere (Q4). The same situation was observed by [WoHa10] and ascribed to the fact that European companies have adopted ISO 9000 more systematically than North American companies.

The world-wide leading process modelling language (Q4) is the BPMN, followed by UML activity diagrams and the event-driven process chain (EPC). An analogous result, but without considering the EPC, was conveyed by the "BPTrends report" [WoHa10]. The BPMN is especially used in European companies as well as in departments for BPM and company organization. Companies from the 'other' countries and IT departments prefer UML activity diagrams over the BPMN. The event-driven process chain is mainly prominent in European companies and in BPM departments. The tools used to describe processes support this dissemination order or process modelling languages (Q11).

Irrespective of the particular process modelling language, the *most needed concepts* to describe business processes are (in decreasing order of importance) the following (Q19): tasks, relationships, persons or roles, documents and resources. The most common relationship types are sequences, AND- or OR-split and merge, whereas looping and XOR-splits are not widespread (Q20), (Q21). Conditions matter for starting tasks or guiding the selection of tasks in splits (Q20). Most conditions refer to the results of adjacent tasks or the overall process state (Q21). In contrast to the importance of time for business processes observed in this investigation so far, time information is not an important condition type (Q21A). With regard to persons or roles, the companies particularly wish to represent capabilities and organizational units (Q23); otherwise, the process descriptions can hardly act as guidelines for persons involved in process execution (Q5). Finally, the prime resource types for business processes are information (immaterial), documents (material), personnel and software systems (Q22), which agrees with the observation that personnel is the third most important concept in process descriptions (Q19).

For the BPMN it was reported that task, sequence flow, start/end event, pool and general/parallel gateway as well as lane and XOR gateway are the construct types most often used, among which XOR-gateways come last [zMRI07], [zMRI08]. Bearing in mind that events are syntactically required by the BPMN, and pool or lane represent persons or roles, this assessment of the BPMN construct types is in line with our results. In contrast to our findings, looping was rated as essential by 42 % of the participants in another investigation [ReIR+06].

When asked about additional concepts not usually provided by process modelling languages, but necessary in order to describe processes (Q24), the companies listed the execution status (of tasks), goals (for processes) and cost (for processes and tasks). These concepts are implied by process monitoring, which was mentioned as a reason to describe processes (Q5). Functional areas in particular have an urgent need for these additional concepts because they rank process monitoring capabilities as the third most important functionality (Q8) for BPM software; see Table 4-25.

Altogether, Table 5-1 shows that our findings are quite well supported – by consistency among the responses to several questions, by statistical significance or by other empirical investigations. Thus it makes sense to discuss the overall implications of our results concerning BPM maturity, which is done in the next section. Finally, Section 5.3 investigates whether or not the most widespread process modelling languages satisfy the description requirements summarized in Table 5-1.

5.2 Current BPM Maturity from the IT Perspective

5.2.1 Measuring BPM Maturity

In general, *maturity* expresses an organization's capabilities or competences within a domain – such as BPM – and is assessed by *maturity models*. Numerous BPM maturity models exist and not all of them have undergone a methodically sound design process [BeKP09]. Table 5-2 summarizes the most popular ones; each of them defines a set of *maturity levels* that cumulatively build on each other and represent certain capabilities. Here we focus in particular on the capabilities related to IT.

The first prominent maturity model was the *Capability Maturity Model (CMM),* the purpose of which was to assess the maturity of software development processes and to stimulate appropriate improvements. In the CMM, software process maturity means "… the extent to which a specific process is explicitly defined, managed, controlled and effective" [PaCC93]. The CMM distinguishes between five *maturity levels* (initial, repeatable, defined, managed and optimizing) that are stages on the evolution path from an immature to a mature organization. Each maturity level is broken down into key process areas. A *key process area* groups several goals that must be accomplished at that level as well as practice in order to achieve these goals [PaCC93].

According to the CMM, a company has a single maturity level at a certain point in time. Being at a maturity level is the precondition for the transition to the next higher maturity level. This *staged view* (also applied by [McJo01]) is unrealistic insofar as it ignores differences in maturity between organizational units or process areas. For this reason the CMM's successor, called *CMMI (Capability Maturity Model Integration)*, added a continuous view where a company can have a distinct capability level and, therefore, maturity for each process area [CMM06].

Neither the CMM nor the CMMI were designed for assessing BPM maturity; nevertheless, the CMMI is occasionally applied for that purpose, e.g. [WoHa10]. More typically, the CMM and CMMI serve as the foundation for specific BPM maturity models, see Table 5-2.

Table 5-2: Selected BPM maturity models

Reference	Maturity levels			Role of IT at distinct BPM maturity levels
	#	Defined by	Assessment	
[PaCC93] CMM	5	Key process areas with goals and best practices for achieving them	Formal	Outside scope
[Harm04]	5	Checklist	Informal	Level 2: Process modelling tools Level 3: Process repository Level 4: IT and processes aligned
[Fisc04]	5	Criteria of levers of change (strategies, controls, people, processes, technologies); checklist	Informal	Level 2: IT integration drives processes Level 4: BPM solutions automate processes Level 5: Process automation and monitoring with business partners
[MeSi06]	6	Criteria for critical success factors (strategic alignment, culture and leadership, people, governance, methods, IT)	Semi-formal	Level 3: Use of BPM suites Level 5: Agile IT services
[McJo01] [McWB+09]	4	Basic components: process view, process jobs, process measurement and management systems. Supporting components: process-structure and customer-focussed process values	(Quantitative)*	Level 3: Process language Level 4: Process management systems
[RoBr05] [RoBH04]	5	Cube with 25 assessment fields; criteria of BPM coverage (number of processes, staff involvement, links to management tools) and proficiency (response to BPM issues, frequency of BPM activities, suitability of BPM tools) for time, scope and separate factors (IT, methods, governance, people, culture, strategic alignment)	(Formal, Quantitative)*	Level 2: Simple process modelling Level 3: Elaborate tools Level 4: Merging of IT and business perspectives on BPM
[LeLK07]	5	Key process areas derived from input, mechanism, control and output of processes	Informal	Not considered
[OMG08] [CuAl06]	5	Key process areas with goals and best practices for achieving them	Formal	Level 2: IT for information -14.1.6.5, SP3 Level 3: IT for transactions - 14.2.9.5, SP6
[Rohl09]	5	Questions for 9 categories: process portfolio & target setting, process documentation, process performance controlling, process optimization, methods & tools, BPM organization, program/data management, qualification, communication, IT architecture	Formal	(Level 3: Processes documented)

Symbols: # Count, * Insufficiently reported

Most BPM maturity models retain the number and names of the levels proposed by the CMM, but complete the derived BPM maturity levels individually. Table 5-3 shows the capabilities that are associated with the maturity levels in the BPM maturity models – insofar as the capabilities occur more than once and are relevant for the use of IT in BPM. The derived *levels of BPM maturity* can be characterized as follows (for the definition of the terms 'BPM tool', 'BPM system' and 'BPM suite' see Section 1):

- *Level 1 (Initial):* (business) processes are not defined or are ad-hoc; the organization is around functional areas, product lines or geographic regions
- *Level 2 (Managed):* some processes are defined (e.g. for core business areas, departments or projects) and documented; general software is used
- *Level 3 (Defined):* all process are defined; BPM is applied with strategic intent; the organization is process-oriented; BPM tools are used; processes are changed reactively
- *Level 4 (Quantitatively managed):* all processes are measured and controlled; BPM and IT are aligned; processes are automated by BPM suites
- *Level 5 (Optimization)*: process automation involves business partners; processes are proactively improved; IT is agile.

Assessing BPM maturity is difficult because most of the capabilities signalling some level of maturity cannot be measured directly; instead, indicators must be used. Simpler BPM maturity models merely provide a set of criteria for each maturity level, e.g. [Harm04]; more sophisticated models group the criteria by levers of change [Fisc04] or success factors ([MeSi06]; [RoBr05]), and some BPM maturity models retain the CMM style [LeLK07] and [OMG08]. The procedure for assessing maturity can be (see Table 5-2):

- *Informal*, if the criteria that have to be checked are rather weakly verbalized;
- *Formal* if the criteria are ordered and associated with best practices (CMM style; [PaCC93] and [OMG08]) or questions [Rohl09], or
- *Quantitative*, if the criteria for the maturity levels involve statistics.

Because of the unavoidable usage of indicators, the measurement of BPM maturity is not unique. Additionally BPM maturity usually involves other factors than IT such as methods, governance, people, culture and strategic alignment [RoBr05]. However, IT has turned out to be the key factor for reaching the higher levels (4 and 5) of BPM maturity [McWB+09]. Consequently, in order to support companies in progressing to these higher levels it can be fruitful to assess their current IT-related BPM maturity.

In order to measure the BPM maturity implied by the results of our survey, we have analyzed the BPM maturity models listed in Table 5-2 and identified the IT-related *capabilities* associated with each BPM maturity level (see Table 5-3). From the results of this analysis we have calculated the *mode* and the *mean BPM maturity* level for each capability; the latter one is used in the tables of Section 4 because it is more selective than the mode.

The answer alternatives from our questionnaire can be seen as indicators that interpret each capability. All answer alternatives are associated with a single capability (and thus BPM maturity level). Some capabilities are the object of parallel questions – in order to increase the reliability of our results.

Most relationships between answers and capabilities in Table 5-3 should be obvious. It is mainly the following interpretations that deserve some explanation. Firstly, office software (Q18) can be used even if a company is not engaged in BPM and does not own any other applications; thus it was rated as an indicator for independent software (maturity level ML = 1). Similarly, the execution of tasks and information providing (Q9) can also be achieved by independent software systems (ML 1). Secondly, the alignment of software with systems (ML = 4) should rely mainly on the prevalent types of applications that are involved in process execution – such as ERP systems and similar; the use of BPM tools or suites is more of an add-on to the existing system landscape than an 'alignment'. Thirdly, we use the postponement of tasks (Q31), i.e. incrementally advancing a process instead of designing it completely in advance, to indicate agile IT (ML = 5) – just as process changes that occur daily or in each execution (Q27). The other maturity levels of Table 4-11 were assigned so that they shrink with decreasing frequency of change. Fourthly, as the maturity levels build on each other, complete process coverage (ML = 3) can be assumed when not only the core processes related to customers and products are described, but also the ones that refer to administration and emergency procedures (Q15) and, thus, do not only support the most popular process goals such as customer satisfaction. Then, the organization is also process-oriented (ML = 3). Finally, if justifications for differentiating between the BPM maturity of distinct answers could not be found, the alternatives were assigned to the same maturity level (*principle of indifference*). The results of our BPM maturity assessment are summarized in the next section.

Table 5-3: BPM maturity from the IT perspective in the literature and the questionnaire

Capabilities		Characterized Maturity Level									Mode	Mean	Interpretation in the Questionnaire (IT view)	
		R1	R2	R3	R4	R5	R6	R7	R8	R9			Quest.	Answer(s)
Organization	Process-oriented	3		3	3	3		3			3	3	Q15	Customer contact; Product
													Q33	1 Company & > 1 Department
	Along value chain, incl. business partners		4	5	5	4	5				5	4.6	Q33	Other Companies
													Q18	Application at business partners; SCM system(s)
IT	Independent software systems			1	1	1	1				1	1	Q18	Office software
													Q9	Execution of tasks; information providing
	Integrated software systems			2				4	4		2;4	3	Q15	Software integration; data transformation
													Q5	Integration of software systems
													Q6	Integration software; data warehouses
													Q18	Integration Software/middleware; database/warehouse(s); product data
	Software systems aligned with processes		4				4				4	4	Q6	ERP and alike
													Q18	ERP; CRM; procurement; production data
	Adaptive, agile IT			5	5						5	5	Q27	Daily; in each execution
													Q31	Postponing the selection of tasks
BPM methodology			2				2		3	3	2	2.5	Q3	Within departments & centrally aligned; BPM team
													Q11	In-house solutions
Analysis	No/ad-hoc processes	1	1			1	1	1	1		1	1	Q30	Next task determined ad-hoc
	Local processes (projects, core business)	2	2		2	2		2	2	2	2	2	Q33	1 Department & > 1 Person
													Q3	In Departments, without alignment
	Complete process coverage	3	3					3		3	3	3	Q15	Administration; emergency procedure(s)
	Standard/"to-be" processes; best practices	3							3	2	3	2.7	Q5	Guidelines
Description	Simple process description					2	2				2	2	Q5	Documentation
													Q4	Text; tables
													Q11	MS Word
	Process modelling		2		2	3	3	3	3	3	3	2.7	Q4	With languages
													Q6	MS Visio; iGrafx; ADONIS; SemTalk
Implementation	BPM suites, automated process execution			4	3	4	3		5		3; 4	3.8	Q5	Automated process execution
													Q11	IBM Websphere; ARIS; Oracle BPM; TIBCO iProcess; Intalio; SAP ECC
													Q18	BPM suites
													Q9	Routing; automated process execution
Monitoring	No measures, unpredictable	1			1	1					1	1	Q10	Nothing
	Measured and controlled	4	4	4	3	3	4	3	3	4	4	3.6	Q5	Monitoring
													Q10	Status; failures; deviations; processors; machines
	Quantitative measures	4	5					4	5	4	4	4.2	Q10	Times, consumed material
Change	Reactive	4				2		3			—	3	Q30	Internal disruptions; deviations from plans; inf. from environment
													Q33	Applying change mechanisms; predefined process variants
	Improvement	5	5	5	6			5	5	5	5	5.1	Q5	Business process reengineering
													Q30	Evolving business

Abbreviated references: R1: [PaCC93], R2: [Harm04], R3: [Fisc04], R4: [MeSi06], R5: [McWB+09], R6: [RoBr06], R7: [LeLK07], R8: [CuAl06], R9: [Rohl09]

5.2.2 IT-related BPM Maturity implied by the Survey

The investigation presented in this book was not primarily conducted to assess BPM maturity. Therefore not all questions of the questionnaire are related to BPM maturity, and the column 'ML' is therefore missing in several tables of Section 4. Basically, the assessment of BPM maturity from the IT perspective concentrates on the nature of business processes (scope, distribution, and stability), process design and monitoring as well as process execution support as these criteria consistently emerged from the analyzed BPM maturity models (see Table 5-3).

Table 5-4 summarizes the questions from the survey that contribute to the IT-related BPM maturity. Per region we give the maturity level that is associated with the answer alternative which represents the mode for this question. The modes are shaded in the Tables of Section 4. In the case of multi-modal answers (framed in Table 5-4), the mean maturity is calculated. The questions for which the regional differences are significant are marked. Altogether a continuous and informal assessment of BPM maturity is adopted, i.e. the levels of BPM maturity can differ for separate questions. The limitations of this BPM maturity assessment are discussed in Section 6.

Table 5-4: BPM maturity from the IT view per region

Question	Content	Maturity Level (ML)		
		North America	Europe	Other
Q15	Process scope	3	3	3
Q33	Distribution of processes	3	3	4.6
Q27	Frequency of process changes	1.5	2	1
Q30**	Reasons for process change	5.1	5.1	3
Q31	Coping with process change	3	3	3
Q3	Organization of process design	2.3	2.5	2.5
Q5**	Reasons for describing processes	5.1	5.1	2.7
Q4**	Style for describing processes	2	2	2
Q11**	Software used to describe and manage processes	2.7	2.7	2
Q6	Process models in non-BPM software	4	4	4
Q18	Applications in process execution	3	3	3
Q9	Required support for process execution	1	1	1
Q10	Information (wished to be) monitored	3.7	3.7	3.7
Total mode (rounded maturity level)		3	3	3
Total mean		3.0	3.1	2.7

** Significant for $\alpha = 0.05$

From the IT perspective, the results of our survey indicate that the companies – irrespective of the region – have on average reached BPM maturity Level 3 (see the mode maturity level in Table 5-4). This average BPM maturity Level of 3 is one stage higher and more settled than the one reported in other empirical investigations, which locate the companies at BPM maturity Level 2 or between the Levels 2 and 3 [WoHa10]. The deviation may be due to the fact that more recent data was used here and that other BPM success factors such as 'people' and 'strategic alignment' were neglected, which can contribute to a lower overall BPM maturity [WoHa10].

While the mode BPM maturity level across all questions is three for each region, the total mean BPM maturity shows some superiority of European and North American companies over companies from 'other' countries. This superiority can also be observed for the significant Questions (Q5), (Q11) and (Q30).

From the results of the research, the following recommendations can be derived: European and North American companies can improve their BPM maturity by involving business partners in their BPM activities (Q33).

The BPM maturity of the companies from 'other' countries will increase when they shift from 'process descriptions as guidelines' to business process reengineering (Q5), use graphical process modelling tools instead of text processing systems (Q11) and change their processes more often (Q27) and in line with the evolving business instead of as a reaction to external forces (Q30).

5.3 Evaluation of Common Process Modelling Languages

5.3.1 Widespread Process Modelling Languages

The most widespread process modelling languages are the BPMN, UML activity diagrams and the even-driven process chain (see Table 4-33). In this section we briefly describe their main constructs as a basis for language assessment in Section 5.3.3. Table 5-5 brings the languages' constructs face to face. Figure 5-1 to Figure 5-3 show a sample process that is modelled with each of the languages. We have used the BPMN Version 1.2 [OMG09], the UML Version 2.1 [OMG07] as well as the extended event-driven process chain [ScTA05], because they were the current ones when the investigation was conducted.

In the *sample process*, a customer configures a product and orders it afterwards. The order management department (of some company) is responsible for all planning and checking all activities related to this order. Firstly, during order processing, the order is read, checked for completeness of all information, and eventually entered into some software application. Afterwards, a technical assessment (to determine whether the customer's configuration of the product is valid and conflict-free) and a credit assessment (to determine whether the customer is creditworthy) must be performed. If both assessments are successful, the order management department releases a production order, which is handed over to manufacturing (where the assembling of the configured product starts). Afterwards, a confirmation of the order is send to the customer by surface mail. If any part of the assessment fails, the order must be rejected and the customer is informed about this rejection by surface mail.

Altogether, the sample process was drawn up with the didactic intention of introducing as many of the constructs of the process modelling languages as possible. Therefore it is not realistic and it contains simplifications and specifics that were necessary in order to comply with the languages' syntax. All diagrams were drawn with Microsoft Visio, demonstrating the language-independence of this application and underpinning its dominant position for process descriptions, Table 4-20 and Table 4-21.

The *Business Process Model and Notation BPMN* [OMG11], which was called Business Process Modelling Notation until Version 1.1 [OMG09], is the most recent and globally dominant (see Table 4-33) process modelling language. The set of core constructs of Version 1.2 is separated into flow objects, connecting objects, 'swimlanes' and artefacts [OMG09].

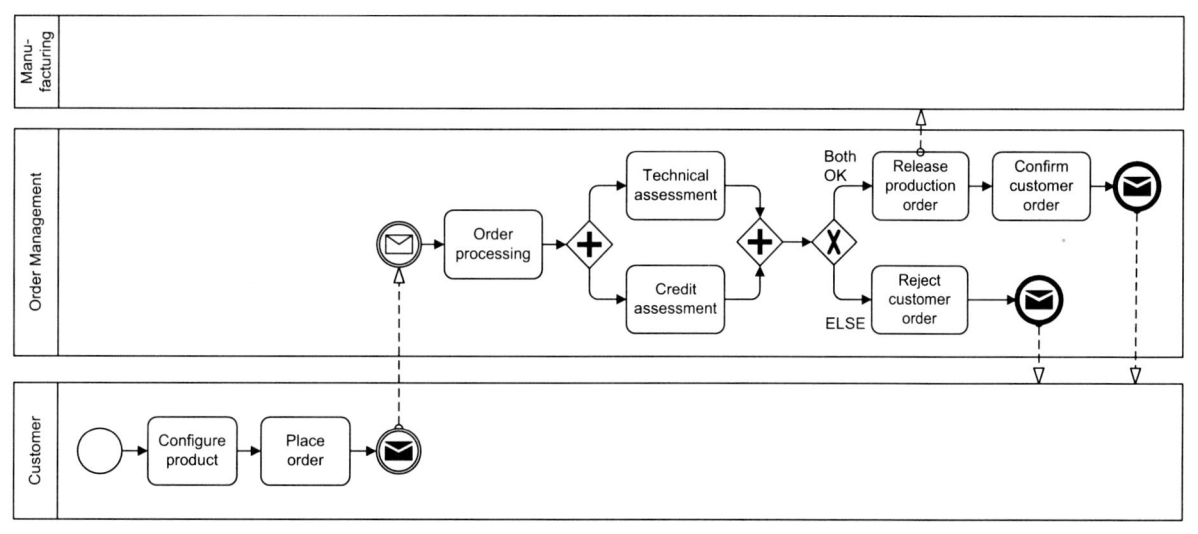

Figure 5-1: Extract of an order management process as BPMN diagram

Flow objects define the behaviour of a process; they comprise activities, gateways and events. An *activity* is the work to be done in a process; it can be atomic (*task*) or non-atomic (*sub-process*). *Gateways*, of which several types exist, control the divergence and the convergence of a process's flow. *Events* are things that happen and influence the flow of a process; they usually have a trigger and a result. A further differentiation is made between *start events* that initiate the process, *end events* which mark that the process is finished and *intermediate events*, which occur between the start and the end event(s).

Connecting objects, i.e. sequence flow, message flow and association, link the flow objects with each other or with other objects. A s*equence flow* shows the order of tasks or activities (*control flow*), whereas the *message flow* indicates which process participants (represented by pools) exchange messages. *Swimlanes* (i.e. pools and their sub-partitions called 'lanes') express responsibilities and capabilities for activities or parts of processes; for example, they can represent participants, organizational units or resources. Finally, *artefacts* provide additional information about the process, but do not influence the control flow. The following artefacts are predefined: data object, group (a box around flow objects) and annotation.

The set of extended constructs of the BPMN contains more specialized flow and connecting objects [OMG09]. For example, *specialized sets* of start, intermediate and end *events* are defined by considering the distinct triggers (of start/intermediate events) and results (of end events), such as messages, timing, errors and rules in the sense of conditions, see Table 5-5. Additionally, sequence flow is stereotyped as normal flow, *conditional flow* (which is associated with a condition and only used when this condition evaluates to 'true' during process execution) and *default flow* (used when none of the conditional flows evaluates to true in some situations). Further, distinct types of *gateways* are provided in order to facilitate the usual splitting and merging of the control flow, namely *parallel* (all outgoing/incoming sequence flows are to be followed; *AND*), *exclusive* (based on some condition, only one out of several outgoing/incoming sequence flows is to be followed; *XOR*) and *inclusive* (all outgoing/incoming sequence flows whose conditions evaluate to true are to be followed; *OR*). The BPMN also supports even more specific gateway types such as complex, data-based or event-based gateways. Finally, compound activities (*sub-processes*), activity *looping* (tasks that are repeated) and *multiple-instance activities* (tasks that are executed several times, possibly simultaneously) are specializations of the core construct *activity*.

BPMN diagrams are mostly drawn from the left to the right, see Figure 5-1. The *BPMN syntax* is fairly simple as most connections between flow objects are allowed. It is only forbidden [OMG09] to draw sequence flows that leave the boundaries of sub-processes or pools, to use message flows within the same pool (message flows can only connect separate pools), to use gateways as start or end of message flows and to use default flows without OR/XOR gateways. Start events for processes are only required when end events are used in these processes, and it is also allowed to start a process from a gateway.

UML activity diagrams [OMG07] have been the antecedence of the BPMN. They are characterized by a large number of constructs and almost no syntactic restrictions. In the following we focus only on the most relevant constructs for the purpose of this book. Figure 5-2 shows the sample process modelled with this language.

The basic constructs of activity diagrams are called *activity nodes*, which are further specialized into executable nodes, control nodes and object nodes [OMG07]. *Executable nodes* do the work in a process; they comprise *activities* (sequenced behavioural parts of a process) and *actions* (atomic steps within an activity). Activities can be structured, for example, to represent *loops* and *conditions*. The sending of a *signal* is a special action type that represents the asynchronous transfer of messages from senders to receivers. Another special action type provides a mechanism for dealing with *timing* events (e.g. durations, points in time).

Control nodes coordinate the order of activities. The most important control nodes are [OMG07] the *initial node* (process start) and the *final node* (ends of activities or flows, respectively), *fork* (split into several concurrent flows; *AND*), *decision* (selection of one out of several outgoing flows; *XOR*), as well as *join* and *merge*, which bring the flows, which were separated by fork and decision, together again. Finally, *object nodes* can store data values. *Exceptions* are special objects for unplanned behaviour.

Activity nodes can be connected by *edges*, which are either control flow or object flow. A *control flow* is an edge that starts an executable or control node after the previous nodes have been finished [OMG07]. *Object flows* are edges that model the flow of data to or from object nodes.

Activities that share characteristics or resources are usually grouped into an *activity partition*; thus these partitions can represent organizational units. Activity partitions can be drawn vertically (such as in Figure 5-2) or horizontally; in the latter case they are very similar to the BPMN 'swimlanes'.

Finally, the *event-driven process chain (EPC)* is the process modelling language with the smallest set of constructs – and the most restrictive syntax [ScTA05]. This process modelling language is mainly used in Europe (see Table 4-33) - and probably known to all users of the ARIS toolset (though this toolset is not restricted to the EPC). The core nodes of an EPC are events, functions and connectors, which are connected by directed edges to

Table 5-5: Main constructs of the most widespread process modelling languages

Semantics	UML Activity Diagrams [OMG07]	Business Process Model and Notation [OMG09]	Event-driven process chain
Tasks	Activity	Task	Function
Control Flow	↓	→	↓
Types of Control Conditions			
AND	Fork: / Join:	✣	∧
OR	—	○ ✳ Conditional flow: ◇→	∨
XOR	Decision, Merge: ◇	⊗	XOR
Loops	(dashed box)	Task ↻ Task ‖‖‖	(Control Flow)
Event	Start: ● End: ⊗ ● Timer: ⌛ Signals: Sending, Receiving Exception: △	Start, Intermediate (Catching, Throwing), End — Message, Timer, Error, Cancel, Compensation, Conditional, Link, Signal, Terminate, Multiple	Event
Responsibilities	Activity Partition	Pool / Lane	Organizational Unit
Resources	Object Node	Data Object	Document; Supporting Object

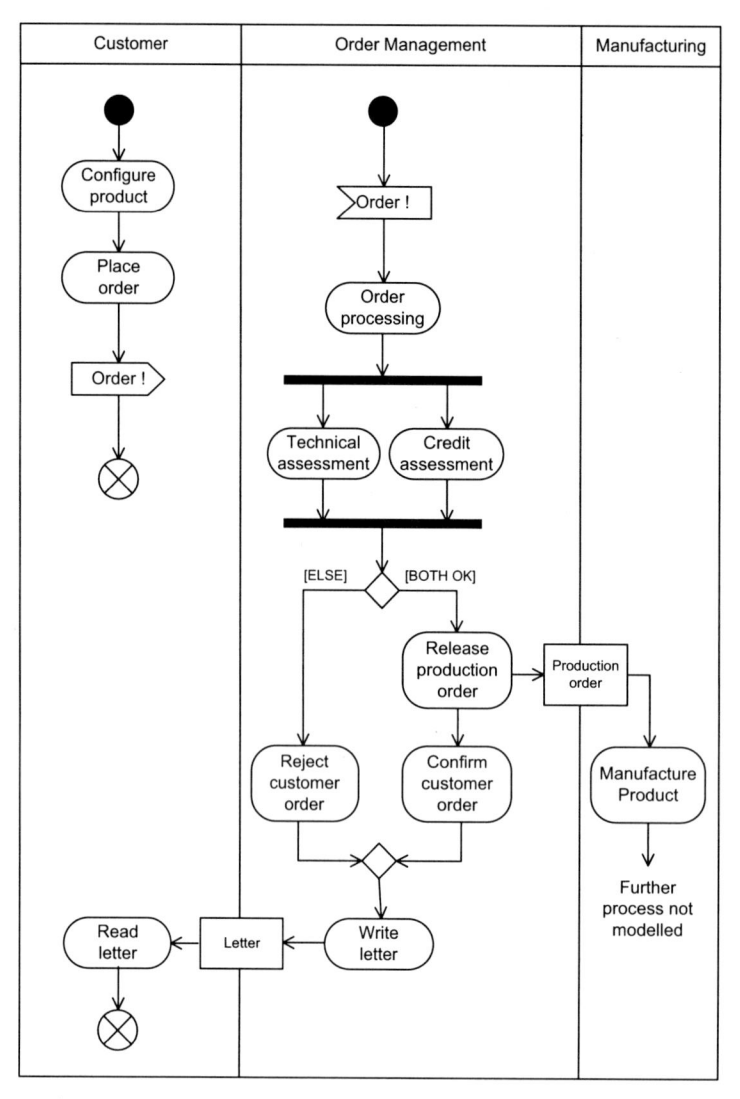

Figure 5-2: Extract of an order management process as UML activity diagram

represent the control flow [ScTA05]. *Events* are passive elements; they describe the conditions to start a function or the state in which a function results. *Functions* are the (time-consuming) activities that must be executed in a process. Finally, *connectors* describe logical relationships between events and functions. The following connector types are predefined: *AND* (all incoming/outgoing flows must be executed), *XOR* (exactly one incoming/outgoing flow must be executed) and *OR* (at least one incoming/outgoing flow must be executed). The connector types can be used both to split and merge the *control flow*, which represents the temporal-logical relationships between events and functions and is depicted vertically in an EPC.

The EPC *syntax* is very restrictive. Functions can have only one incoming and outgoing flow and are usually connected either to an event or to a connector; however, in strict sequences (see Figure 5-3) direct connections between functions are allowed in order to omit 'trivial events' [Seid10]. Events cannot have more than one incoming or outgoing flow and can only be connected to functions or connectors. Additionally, a process must be started from and finished by events. If more than one flow goes to or from a function or an event, connectors must be used. A connector can be connected to another connector; splitting and merging of a process path should use the same connector.

The constructs listed so far belong to the basic EPC. Figure 5-3 shows the sample process as an extended event-driven process chain. An *extended EPC* (*eEPC*) additionally provides, for example, organizational units, supporting objects, documents and *goals* [ScTA05]. All of these additional constructs can only be assigned to functions. *Organizational units* represent the persons responsible for a function. *Supporting objects* (various symbols exist) reflect the 'real world' input or output of functions such as electronic information, machines, hardware and software application. Finally, *documents* are non-electronic information that is passed around. Altogether, the additional constructs of the extended EPC are quite adaptive to the modeller's needs.

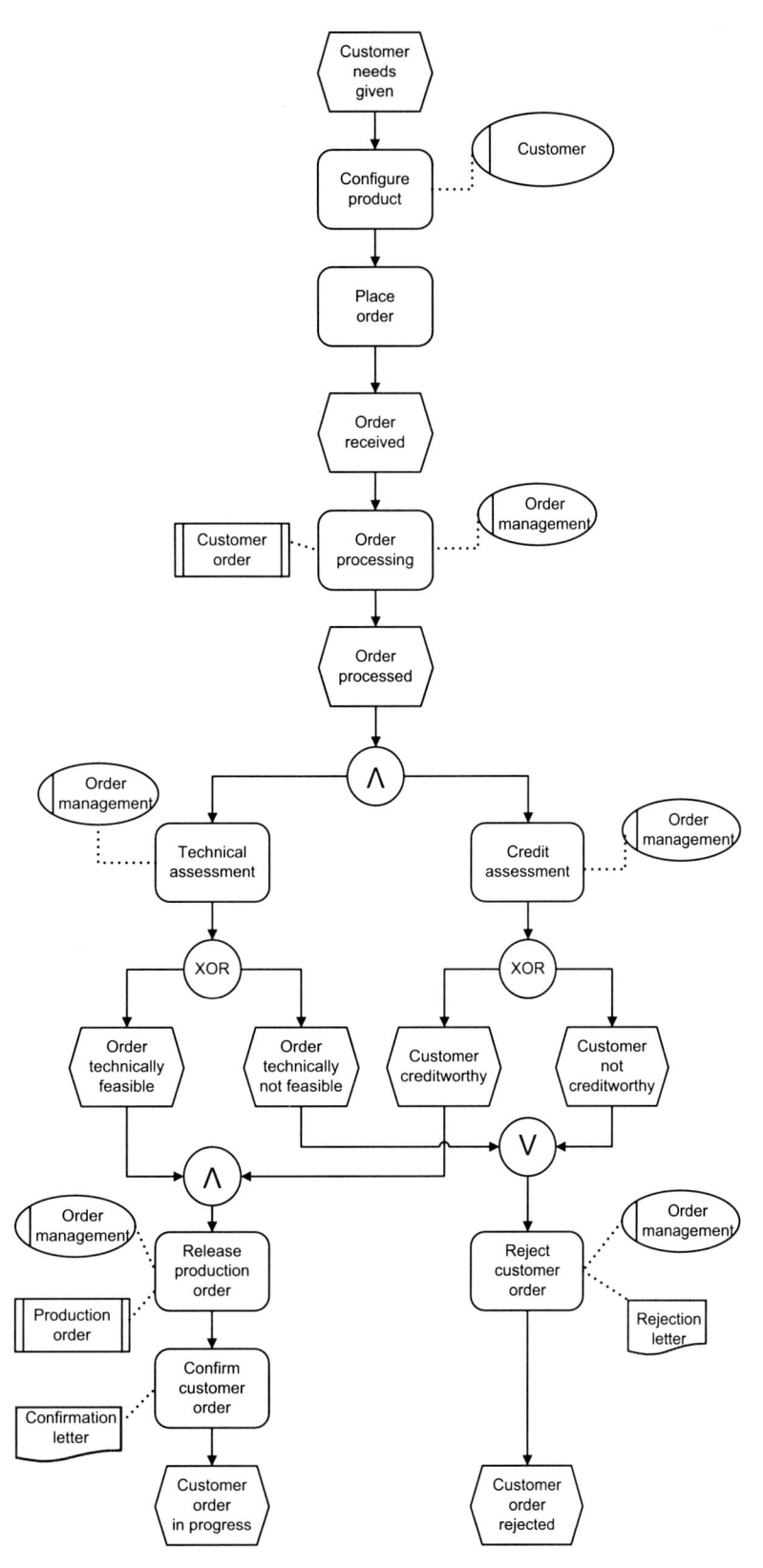

Figure 5-3: Extract of an order management process as extended Event-driven process chain

Though the graphical symbols used by the process modelling languages and the created diagrams look different, Table 5-5 shows some kind of agreement in the basic, process-related semantics. The differences and commonalities between the process modelling languages in the light of our empirical investigation are discussed in depth in Section 5.3.3. Before that, Section 5.3.2 summarizes prominent approaches to assess process modelling languages.

5.3.2 Survey-based Assessment of Evaluation Frameworks

The number of process modelling languages has been constantly increasing over the last twenty years. As companies need guidelines in order to select a process modelling language (and researchers need justifications to invent yet another one), several evaluations and comparisons of process modelling languages have been proposed. These evaluations aim at identifying the 'best' process modelling language in terms of expressiveness, understandability (e.g. [MeRC07], [ReDr07]) or complexity (e.g. [ReMS+09]). The current evaluations of the expressiveness of process modelling languages are particularly misleading since the underlying evaluation frameworks are based on theoretical considerations instead of the companies' requirements. This will become obvious in the following.

Expressiveness means the ability to represent any meaning required to accomplish some purpose, and it is usually assessed on the basis of a reference [Pati04]. In the field of process modelling languages, two *types of references* can be identified (see Table 5-6): widespread evaluation frameworks such as the Bunge-Wand-Weber (BWW) representation model and workflow patterns, which are mostly complementary [ReRK07], and new evaluation frameworks. *Widespread evaluation frameworks* are used thoroughly in the BPM community. The *Bunge-Wand-Weber representation model* is a philosophically based ontology relating to things that exist in the real world, their properties, states and their coupling with each other [GrRo00]. As the BWW representation model is not especially targeted at BPM, the terms used therein are general and not easy to interpret. In contrast, *workflow patterns* spring from the BPM community; these are stereotyped, language-neutral and tool-neutral concepts related to the control flow, resources, data and exception handling in processes [RuHA+06]. As can be seen from Table 5-6, the number of workflow patterns is huge, and the distinctions between the individual patterns are therefore not easy to grasp. Additionally, because they were generalized from existing workflow management systems, many patterns have an implementation background and therefore are not really needed in order to *conceptually* describe a business process for organizational purposes. In order to remedy the deficiencies of the BWW representation model and the workflow patterns, some new evaluation frameworks have been proposed, inspired by the process modelling literature (e.g. [LiKo06], [SöAJ+02]) or BPM methods [LiYP02].

Any type of reference is created to finally contrast it with process modelling languages. The result of the comparison usually shows some *misfit*, which can be of the following *types* [Webe97]:

- *Incompleteness*: Concepts from the reference are not supported by the process modelling language.

- *Excess*: The process modelling language provides concepts that are not contained in the reference.

- *Redundancy*: The same concept of the reference is represented by more than one construct of the process modelling language.

- *Overload*: A construct from the process modelling language represents several concepts of the reference.

Some papers that report evaluations of process modelling languages list the languages' incomplete, excess, redundant or overloaded constructs (e.g. [GrRo00]), whilst other papers use tables to comment accordingly on the constructs [SöAJ+02] or mark satisfied, unsatisfied and partially satisfied requirements of the reference (e.g. [RuHA+06], [LiKo06], [LiYP02]).

Taken as a whole, the results are mostly devastating as they confirm the obviously insufficient expressiveness of the existing process modelling languages. However, companies should only be worried about this assessment if the references used to assess expressiveness truly reflected their expressiveness requirements – which is not the case (see Table 5-6).

The first column of Table 5-6 summarizes the companies' requirements for process descriptions based on the Questions (Q19) to (Q24) of our investigation. The order of the concepts in bold print basically corresponds to the ranks from Table 4-38; deviations, which were necessary in order to evaluate expressiveness, are explained in Section 5.3.3.

For all evaluation frameworks, it is marked in Table 5-6 whether these consider each requirement directly, indirectly or not at all. *Direct consideration* means that a requirement is mentioned in the framework – either verbatim or synonymously; the synonyms are given in Table 5-6. In the case of an *indirect consideration* some requirement follows from other requirements.

Table 5-6. Considered requirements in prominent evaluation frameworks for process modelling languages

Our empirical results Concepts required to describe processes (Q19)	Evaluation frameworks				
	Newly proposed			Widespread	
	[LiYP02]	[SöAJ+02]	[LiKo06]	BWW [GrRo00]	Workflow pattern [vAtH10]
Tasks	Activity	Activity	Activity	Transformation	♦
Relationships between tasks (Q20)	Relation	Dependency	Control flow	State law	♦
Sequence	Relation	✓	Control flow	♦ State law	WFCP-1
Start Condition (of task)	(Behaviour)	♦	—	Lawful transformation	WFDP-33, 34, 35, 38, 39
Split (Q21)	♦ Relation	♦	✓	♦ State law	WFCP-2, 6
AND		Fork	✓		WFCP-2
OR		Selection	✓		WFCP-6
XOR		Selection	✓		WFCP-4
Merge		✓	Join		WFCP-3, 5, 7, 8, 9, 30 to 38
Loop		—	Control flow	—	WFCP-10, 21
Persons or Roles (Q23)	Agent	Role	Participant	Thing	R-RBA
Capability	♦	♦	Role	Property	R-CBA, R-DE
Organizational Unit	♦	♦	✓	Thing	R-OA
Name	—	(Actor)	✓	Property	R-DBAS
Documents or objects	Entity, Information	Information	Data Object	Thing	WFDP-2, 3, 5, 6
Events (Q17)	✓	✓	✓	✓	WFDP-37
Information/Massage	✓	♦	♦	♦	WFDP-1, 5, 6, 8 to 14, 16 to 18, 20 to 22, 24, 25, 38
Timing	♦	✓	♦	♦	(WFEH Deadline)
Human intervention	♦	♦	♦	♦	WFDP-7, 14 to 25 (WFCP-16; WFEH External trigger)
State of process/tasks	♦	State	♦	State	(WFDP-38;WFEH)
Deviations	♦	♦	♦	♦	WFEH (except for External Trigger)
(Additional**) Resources (Q22)	✓	✓	✓	Thing	R-DA, -FBA, -RA, -CH, -RF, -HBA, -DBOS, -DBOM, -RMA, -RRA, -SHQ, -ED, -LD, -D, -E, -SD, -AR
Software Systems	Information	♦	Application	Thing	♦
Machines, Appliances	Entity	♦	Resource	Thing	♦
Additional information for a task (Q24)					
Execution status	—	State	—	State	WFDP-1, (WFDP-3)
Priority	—	—	—	Property	
Goal	—	✓	✓	Property	
Cost	—	—	—	Property	
Excess requirements in the evaluation frameworks					
	—	3	≈ 15	≈ 20	≈ 55

Legend: ✓ Directly considered ♦ Indirectly considered —: Not considered
** Only if not already listed before.

Abbreviations: R: Workflow resource pattern, WFCP: Workflow control pattern, WFDP: Workflow data pattern, WFEH: Workflow exception handling pattern

It becomes apparent that several core requirements to describe processes such as tasks (activities), events and resources are part of all evaluation frameworks, and almost the same terms are used. Other core requirements, e.g. relationships between tasks, persons or roles and documents/objects, also appear in all evaluation frameworks, but the wording varies considerably. In particular, the required details of the core concepts – such as types of relationships or events and information about persons – are often only indirectly considered in the evaluation frameworks. On the other hand, the evaluation frameworks, especially the workflow patterns, consider far more requirements than are actually raised by the companies. This is due to the fact that workflow patterns basically aim at process automation, which is not the companies' main reason for describing processes (see Table 4-31).

The assessment of expressiveness depends on the used reference, which in turn is dictated by the purpose of describing processes and the resulting requirements. The first column of Table 5-6 shows the companies' requirements concerning expressiveness. If we take these requirements as a 'reference' to assess the existing evaluation frameworks, we denote considerable overload and excess. For example, the distinct relationship types required by the companies are not differentiated, but subsumed under the generic requirements 'relation' [LiYP02] or 'state law' [GrRo00]; thus these requirements are *overloaded*. Moreover, the approximate number of *excess requirements* in the evaluation frameworks is shown in the last row of Table 5-6. On the positive side, *incompleteness* concerns only the additional information for tasks, which is mostly not considered in the evaluation frameworks; and *redundancy* is almost no issue (only for documents in [LiYP02]).

Altogether, because of excess and overloaded requirements, the discussed evaluation frameworks for process modelling languages do not adequately reflect the companies' needs concerning expressiveness. Consequently, the published evaluation results concerning the expressiveness of process modelling languages are irrelevant for the companies. In the next section we use the findings of our investigation to provide a realistic evaluation of the most prominent process modelling languages.

5.3.3 Survey-based Comparison of Process Modelling Languages

Basically, expressiveness is the ability to represent any required concept. For process modelling languages these requirements can be seen from the answers to the Questions (Q19) to (Q24) of the survey and are depicted in the first column of Table 5-7. The order of the concepts in bold print corresponds to the ranks from Table 4-38. Most of these concepts were investigated in more detail by further questions, whose numbers are given and whose rankings determine the order of the rows in regular font.

Expressiveness can be quantitatively measured based on a reference. *Valid references* for expressiveness must be consistent sets of independent, atomic statements [Pati04]. In order to serve as a valid reference, redundancy of required concepts (which is the opposite of independence between the statements) was to be avoided. Therefore the first column of Table 5-7 differs from the tables in Section 4 as follows:

- The most important *resources* are information, documents and personnel (see Table 4-48). Persons/roles and documents are listed separately in Table 5-7 – according to Table 4-38. Information that is not a document corresponds to an event (see Table 4-7) and is treated there.

- *Time information* related to tasks and *timely distances* (see Table 4-38) are represented by timing events (see also [OMG07]).

- The resource '*material*' (see Table 4-48) is subsumed under 'object' in Table 5-7.

Since the first column of Table 5-7 is now a valid reference for measuring expressiveness, each line (except for 'Additional information for a task', which is a heading) corresponds to a *reference item*, i.e. an atomic, independent statement. *Expressiveness* can then be *calculated* by relating the sum of all expressible reference items to the sum of all reference items [Pati04].

A reference item counts as *expressible* (count = 1) if a process modelling language directly or indirectly supports it. *Direct support* means that the process modelling language provides a construct that readily represents the semantics of the reference item, whereas *indirect support* requires the combination or appropriate definition of existing constructs to represent these semantics.

Table 5-7. Expressiveness of prominent process modelling languages

Our empirical results Concepts required to describe processes (Q19)	Existing process modelling languages			Standards	
	BPMN 1.2 [OMG09]	UML Activity 2.1 [OMG07]	EPC for ARIS [ScTA05]	WfMC [WfMC95]	XPDL [WfMC08]
Tasks	✓	✓	✓	Activity	Activity
Relationships between tasks (Q20)	✓	✓	✓	Transition condition	Transition
Sequence	✓	✓	✓	Transition	Transition
Start Condition (of task)	♦	✓	♦	Precondition	Transition condition
Split (Q21)	✓	✓	✓	Transition condition	Routing Activity
AND	✓	✓	✓		
OR	✓	—	✓		
XOR	✓	✓	✓		
Merge	✓	✓	✓		
Loop	✓	✓	♦		♦
Persons or Roles (Q23)	✓	✓	♦	Role	Participant, Pool
Capability	♦	♦	♦	♦	Participant
Organizational Unit	♦	♦	✓	♦	Participant, Pool
Name	P	♦	♦	♦	Participant
Documents or objects	♦ *	✓	✓	WF-relevant data	(Data Object)
Events (Q17)	✓	♦	✓	♦	✓
Information/Message	✓	♦	✓	WF-relevant data	Message
Timing	✓	♦	♦	♦	Timer
Human intervention	♦	♦	♦	—	—
State of process/tasks	♦	♦	♦	♦	♦
Deviations	✓	✓	♦	♦	Error
(Additional) Resources (Q22)**	✓	✓	✓	—	♦
Software Systems	♦	♦	✓	Invoked application	Application
Machines, Appliances	♦	♦	✓	—	Participant
Additional information for a task (Q24)					
Execution status	♦	♦ P/S	—	✓	♦ (Extension Attribute)
Priority	♦ P	♦ P/S	—	P	
Goal	♦ P	♦ P/S	✓	—	
Cost	♦ P	♦ P/S	—	—	
Excess constructs or elements provided by the process modelling languages					
	≈ 25	≈ 10	—	—	9
Expressiveness Core/Total Reference					
	1 / 1	0.95 / 0.96	1 / 0.89		

Legend: ✓ Directly supported (count: 1) ♦ Indirectly supported (count: 1) —: Not supported (count: 0)
* No influence on control flow.
** Only if not already listed before; rearrangement due to the calculation of expressiveness (see text).

Abbreviations: P: Property, S: Stereotype, WF: Workflow

The explanations in Section 5.3.1 should make it quite obvious how the most common process modelling languages support the companies' expressiveness requirements, especially as Table 5-5 already provides a comparison of the constructs and partially uses the names of the reference items. The following explanations are intended to further increase clarity.

Many concepts that companies require to describe their processes are directly supported by the considered process modelling languages, even if the names of the language constructs vary. For example, 'control flow' from Table 5-5 is called 'relationship between tasks' in Table 5-7, and it is usually a sequence. The AND/OR/XOR control conditions given in Table 5-5 can be used both to split and merge the control flow. Responsibilities (see Table 5-5) are associated with persons or roles. Documents are resources (see Table 5-5) that can be directly modelled in an EPC as well as in UML activity diagrams ('object nodes'); the 'data object' of the BPMN only indirectly supports documents because it cannot influence the control flow.

Indirect support by adapting more *generic constructs* is very common for the specific reference items. For example, the generic constructs 'pool' and 'lane' of the BPMN and 'activity partition' of UML Activity Diagrams (see Section 5.3.1) can express organizational units, capabilities or even names. The generic construct 'event' of the EPC can represent all specific event types such as messages, timing etc. – as well as conditions.

Information as an event can be modelled in UML activity diagrams by the transfer of object nodes or by signals. Human intervention and states of tasks or processes are indirectly supported in all process model languages, e.g., by conditions or signals (UML), rule/error/multiple events (BPMN) or general events (EPC). Deviations often correspond to exceptions or error situations, for which predefined or generic event types exist in all process modelling languages. In an EPC, the 'supporting object' can comprise software systems, machines or appliances; in the BPMN and UML activity diagrams 'swimlanes' or 'activity partitions' must be used in order to model these resources. Finally, both the UML and the BPMN provide extension mechanisms such as the definition of additional properties or construct specializations (*stereotypes*) that are useful for expressing the additional information for a task (indirect support because of the necessity to extend the process modelling language). With these explanations, the markings for direct and indirect support in Table 5-7 should be comprehensible.

The *total reference* of Table 5-7 consists of 28 items; the line 'Additional information for a task' is a heading and is therefore not counted. If the additional information for a task is excluded, 24 items remain in the *core reference*. For the core reference, the BPMN and the EPC are equally expressive; UML activity diagrams lag behind because of their inability to express OR-splits or joins (see Table 5-7). For the total reference, the BPMN is the most expressive process modelling language, followed by UML activity diagrams and the EPC. The latter one especially suffers from incompleteness (see Section 5.3.2) concerning the additional information about tasks – while the 'winning' languages benefit from their extension mechanisms.

Altogether, the differences in expressiveness are marginal. For the companies this result implies that the BPMN, the EPC and UML Activity Diagrams are interchangeable. Technically, this interchangeability is (except for events that represent human intervention) supported by the *XML Process Definition Language* (XPDL) [WfMC08], a standard for the exchange of process descriptions between tools; see Table 5-7. The XPDL support covers the total reference since additional information for tasks can be defined by 'extension attributes'.

In the process modelling languages construct *overload* (see Section 5.3.2) confines itself to situations were generic constructs such as 'pool', 'activity partition' or 'event' are used in order to indirectly support specific reference items (see above). Construct *redundancy* (see Section 5.3.2) does not occur as it increases the overall number of constructs and thus complexity.

If the *complexity* of a process modelling language is measured by the count of constructs that do *not* represent a reference item ('excess constructs' in Table 5-7), our findings support the greater complexity of the BPMN compared to UML Activity Diagrams as reported in [ReMS+09]. This complexity becomes even worse for the BPMN in Version 2.0, in which the number of constructs has dramatically increased.

To summarize, the most widespread process modelling languages equally satisfy the companies' expressiveness requirements for process descriptions. Thus our evaluation of process modelling languages is far more positive than the existing ones (see Section 5.3.2). This can be attributed to two circumstances: firstly, our reference is restricted to the companies' actual modelling requirements, and thus does not suffer from 'excess requirements' as observed in Section 5.3.2. Secondly, requirements depend on the purpose pursued and dictate the reference that must be used to assess expressiveness. At the present point in time, the most important reasons stated by the companies for describing their business processes are business process reengineering, documentation and guidelines for human process execution (see Table 4-31). Our reference in Table 5-7 is aligned with these purposes. However, if processes are described for the purpose of process automation, more precision and technical details are required, which must be added to the reference; the workflow patterns mentioned in Section 5.3.2 follow this tack. The evaluation of the process modelling languages' expressiveness will then yield deviating results [RuHA+06].

The findings of the empirical investigation presented in this book suggest that the modelling of processes for the companies' most urgent BPM aims requires far less than the workflow patterns, but more than the WfMC reference model [WfMC95], which in fact corresponds to the 'least common denominator' of process description requirements, see Table 5-7.

Altogether, these results concerning the expressiveness of process modelling languages explain why language adaptability and alignment to standards are almost unimportant requirements (see Table 4-24) – in particular because the companies' most urgent, standard requirements concerning process descriptions can be represented with all process modelling languages.

6 Limitations of the Investigation

This investigation was conducted thoroughly. The questionnaire was systematically derived from BPM literature and designed to maximize the reliability of the results; core ideas in particular were explored by more than one question. The participants were sampled by random numbers from the population of the 'Forbes Global 2000' list. All efforts were made to avoid errors during data handling and statistical evaluation. Moreover, the discussion in Section 5.1 has demonstrated the plausibility of the results obtained since they are consistent with each other and with the findings of other empirical investigations. Nevertheless, some limitations exist in relation to the participants, methodical aspects, and the interpretation of BPM maturity as well as expressiveness.

Participants: Because of the sampling procedure (see Section 3.3), the results can be assumed to be valid for large companies that operate worldwide, regardless of their sector. However, the focus on *large companies* is accompanied by some *lack of selectivity*. Most of the investigated companies encompass fairly independent sub-organizations that often use distinct software or process modelling languages. As the majority of our participants had a company-wide picture of the processes (see Table 3-3), the impression of 'anything goes' arises at the company level. This problem affects all investigations of large companies. However, the resulting impression of BPM in practice is quite realistic.

The *Forbes Global 2000* list that constitutes the population of our investigations suffers from three limitations that might well affect the validity of the results. Firstly, it disregards large non-American companies that do not have commercial relations with the USA. Secondly, ranking companies based on sales, profit and market value favours sectors where borrowed capital is important (e.g. banking and insurance companies). Thirdly, non-profit organizations (i.e. public administration, universities) are completely excluded.

Half of our participants work for *IT departments* (see Table 3-2). The resulting IT focus is in line with the research goals of this investigation – and is not restrictive, since the vast majority of the participants had a company-wide picture of the processes (see Table 3-3). Moreover, the findings concerning the reasons for describing processes (see Table 4-31) and the functionalities and qualities required from software (see Table 4-25) in particular show that the role of IT was not overemphasized.

Methodical issues: Numerous questions in the questionnaire required the participants to rate the answer alternatives on various scales (see Section 3.2). Naturally, these *ratings* are *subjective*, which is a common limitation of such surveys. From a methodical point of view, the calculation of *mean ratings* is only valid if the underlying rating levels are equidistant (interval scale). This assumption is generally made [Jack09]. Moreover, our conclusions are derived from the *orders* of the calculated mean ratings and, therefore, remain on ordinal scale. Additionally, the mode was used wherever appropriate because it is a valid descriptive statistic for nominal and ordinal data and is insensitive to outliers [GrWa09].

Question (Q34) required the participants to enter *numerical data values*. It must be assumed that these values are estimates rather than the results of measurements in the companies. Consequently, the findings reported in Section 4.2 should not be taken literally, but considered by magnitude. For this reason no statistical tests were applied to the calculated mean values of Table 4-2. Yet the comparison with the answers to other questions and investigations show (see Table 5-1) shows that our results are plausible.

BPM maturity: The maturity levels used in the tables of Section 4 are the means calculated across several BPM maturity models (see Table 5-3) and are therefore consensual. Nevertheless, two sources of subjectivity can be identified. Firstly, the analyzed BPM maturity models of Table 5-2 contain subjectivity [BeKP09]. Secondly, associating answer alternatives from the questionnaire with capabilities of distinct maturity levels is also a matter of interpretation. Even though most associations between capabilities and answer alternatives in Table 5-3 are quite obvious and the remaining ones were justified, some subjectivity remains.

The total mean and mode BPM maturity level calculated per region in Table 5-4 are probably affected by correlation between the questions. However, the higher BPM maturity of companies from North America and Europe compared to companies from 'other' countries still becomes apparent when considering only the significant questions (Q30), (Q5) and (Q11), which are quite independent.

The overall statement of the regions' BPM maturity must be *put into perspective* since the investigation presented in this book was not intended as a comprehensive BPM maturity assessment and, therefore, discounts all success factors other than IT that contribute to BPM maturity (e.g. people, culture, strategic alignment).

Expressiveness: Process modelling can serve different purposes; the most important ones currently for companies are business process reengineering, documentation and creating guidelines for the people involved in process execution (see Table 4-31). These purposes need expressiveness concerning *description*, which was measured by the reference (first column of Table 5-7) in Section 5.3.3. Distinct purposes such as automated process execution require other expressiveness, i.e. another reference. Consequently, the evaluation of language expressiveness will yield deviating results.

7 Conclusions

This investigation pursued three goals: the exploration of the current usage of software throughout the BPM life cycle, the identification of the companies' requirements concerning software for BPM and the identification of the companies' requirements concerning process modelling languages.

The *current usage of software for BPM* indicates that the worldwide BPM maturity of large companies amounts to Level 3 from the IT perspective. Thus BPM is applied with strategic intent, all processes are defined and BPM tools are used. BPM tools correspond to software that enables process description and analysis to be carried out. Process automation is not a characteristic of BPM maturity Level 3. Consequently, BPM systems are not widespread. Instead, general software such as databases, ERP and CRM systems as well as office tools are used to support process execution. The resulting system landscapes become rather complex, especially since average business processes involve about four departments and one to two business partners, and rely on about four software applications.

Keeping this complexity in mind, the *companies' requirements for BPM software* are quite natural: usability in the sense of obvious, easy-to-learn and efficient human-computer interaction (to support the persons who execute the business processes in place of BPM systems); modelling capabilities (as process models are distinctive at BPM maturity Level 3); report generation (to keep track of the business process in spite of its distribution over organizational and technical units) and software integration (to build a process from the isolated applications). The slow diffusion of BPM systems and suites can probably be attributed to the fact that they do not sufficiently support these requirements – since functionalities and qualities are the most important criteria for the companies in selecting software for BPM, well ahead of pricing.

Process modelling is a key turning point for the transition to BPM maturity Level 3. Since this level is reached by the majority of companies, at least from the IT perspective, their *requirements concerning process modelling* must be satisfied by the current process modelling languages. Indeed, the most common process modelling languages – the BPMN, UML activity diagrams and the EPC – are largely equally *expressive*, i.e., they provide all concepts needed by the companies to describe their business processes. This result has two implications. Firstly, language adaptability is no longer a necessity. Secondly, the mentioned process modelling languages are interchangeable. This interchangeability is even completely supported technically by the XPDL. Consequently, modellers can choose their preferred process modelling language and BPM tool.

Research on the 'best' process modelling language in terms of *understandability* has just started [MeRC07], [ReDr07]. Though no definite answer can yet be given, initial findings indicate that all process modelling languages are equally understandable as far as the common notion of 'business process' is concerned [ReDr07]. If the requirements gathered in this investigation correspond to this common notion, then the most common process modelling languages should be equally understandable – but this is a topic for future research.

Understandability is affected by the number of constructs to reach a distinct expressiveness, and the most prominent process modelling languages differ in the size of the construct vocabulary. If *complexity* is measured by the number of language constructs [ReMS+09], then the BPMN is the most complex and the EPC is the simplest process modelling language; UML activity diagrams lie in between.

The observed equal expressiveness of the considered process modelling languages is only valid for the current most important reasons for describing processes: business process reengineering, documentation and guidelines for process execution. If these reasons change, and this will happen when the companies progress to higher levels of BPM maturity that claim process automation, the expressiveness required will change as well and the process modelling languages will have to evolve. A new investigation will then be necessary to gather the companies' requirements again. In the meantime, every effort should be made to satisfy the current requirements of BPM by designing and using appropriate software.

APPENDIX A: QUESTIONNAIRE

SECTION I - CURRENT STATUS OF PROCESS MANAGEMENT IN YOUR COMPANY
1. What is the business of your department? * ☐ IT ☐ Business Process Management ☐ Company Organization ☐ Functional Area (Purchasing, Sales & Distribution, R&D, etc.) ☐ Product Division
2. Which processes do you know in your company? ♦ * ☐ I know the processes of my own department ☐ I know the processes of other departments ☐ I have a company-wide picture of the processes Other: ………………………………………………………………….. ♦ We assume that your answers to our questions refer to that kind of knowledge.
3. How is process modelling organized in your company? * ☐ Processes are identified and modelled within the individual departments without central coordination ☐ Processes are identified and modelled within the individual departments and then centrally aligned ☐ Process identification and modelling are done by a central process management team Other: ……………………………………………………………………..
4. How do you describe the processes in your company/department? * ☐ As text in normal language ☐ As tables ☐ By using a (process) modelling language, e.g.: ☐ BPEL (Business Process Execution Language) ☐ BPMN (Business Process Modelling Notation) ☐ EPC (Event-driven Process Chain) ☐ IDEF language family ☐ UML (Unified Modelling Language) ☐ Other (process) modelling language, please specify: Other: ……………………………………………………………………..
5. Why do you describe processes in your company/department? * ☐ To document what happens ☐ To have precise, written guidelines for the persons executing the process ☐ To automate the execution of the process, e.g., by software or machine systems ☐ To have targets in monitoring the execution of the processes ☐ To prepare the optimization and reorganization of the processes (business process reengineering) ☐ ISO Certification ☐ To integrate software systems ☐ To select among application systems (by comparing the processes these systems support to the actual processes in our company) Other: …………………………………………………………………….
6. Are process models or workflows part of "other" (i.e. non-BPM) software you use? ♦ * ☐ No ☐ Yes (click below which software) ☐ Integration software (EAI, middleware) ☐ Enterprise resource planning systems ☐ Requirements engineering software ☐ Data Warehouses Other: …………………………………………………………………… ♦ **Process model**: A description of a process at the type level by using some dedicated process modelling language. **Workflow**: A computerized facilitation or automation of a (business) process, in whole or in part.
* Please choose all that apply

[Only answer this question if you answered to question Q6]
7. What is the role of the process models or workflows in this software? *

☐ Routing of tasks to responsible persons
☐ Specification of message flow
☐ Definition of data transformations
☐ Adaptation or configuration of software
Other: ....

SECTION II - TOOLS FOR PROCESS MODELLING AND PROCESS MANAGEMENT

8. Please assess the importance of the following functionalities and qualities for software that supports process management: ♦

	Very Important	Important	Not so important	Not at all important	Don't know
Modelling capabilities	☐	☐	☐	☐	☐
Syntax checks of models with respect to the modelling language	☐	☐	☐	☐	☐
Formal proofs of model correctness	☐	☐	☐	☐	☐
Adaptability of the modelling language	☐	☐	☐	☐	☐
Support for different notations and standards (e.g. BPMN, UML)	☐	☐	☐	☐	☐
Alignment to standards	☐	☐	☐	☐	☐
Simulation of process execution	☐	☐	☐	☐	☐
Process execution or execution support (= workflow enactment)	☐	☐	☐	☐	☐
Monitoring of process execution	☐	☐	☐	☐	☐
Report generation capabilities	☐	☐	☐	☐	☐
Integration of other application software	☐	☐	☐	☐	☐
Usability and user interface	☐	☐	☐	☐	☐

♦ **Enactment:** Interpretation of a process description by some software system; instantiation of processes and sequencing of activities, adding tasks to user work lists, invoking application systems as necessary.

8A. Which other functionality or quality for software that supports process management do you consider important? Please write your answer here:
....

9. How should software support you in the execution of your processes?

	Very Important	Important	Not so important	Not at all important	Don't know
The processes should be totally automated without any human participation	☐	☐	☐	☐	☐
Software executes most of the tasks and guarantees that their order is kept. However, some human interaction is required	☐	☐	☐	☐	☐
Software does not execute tasks, but only routes them to the responsible persons	☐	☐	☐	☐	☐
The tasks of the process and their order are determined by the persons in charge. Software only provides these persons with the information needed to solve the tasks	☐	☐	☐	☐	☐

9A. How should otherwise software support you in the execution of your processes?
Please write your answer here:
....

* Please choose all that apply

[Only answer this question if you answered to question Q9]
9B. During the computerized execution of your processes, in which situations is human interaction required? *

☐ To start the process
☐ To enter new information
☐ To select the next task out of several ones
☐ To approve tasks
Other: ……………………………………………………………………

10. What kind of information do you want to monitor during the execution of a process? *

☐ Nothing
☐ The execution status of a task or a process
☐ Times (waiting times, execution duration)
☐ Machines occupied
☐ Failures in process execution
☐ Tasks' processors
☐ Consumed material
☐ Deviations from the process model
Other: ……………………………………………………………………

11. Which tool do you currently use to describe or manage your processes? *

☐ ARIS Toolset of IDS Scheer
☐ ADONIS of BOC Group
☐ Bonapart of Pykos Gmbh
☐ Holocentric Modeler
☐ iGrafx Suite from iGrafx
☐ Income Suite
☐ Intalio BPMS
☐ iProcess tools of TIBCO
☐ Prometheus Suite from ibo Software
☐ SAP R/3 or mySAP ECC (Workflow Component)
☐ Semtalk of Semtation Gmbh
☐ Visio of Microsoft Corp.
☐ Websphere from IBM
☐ Word of Microsoft Corp. or other text processing systems
☐ In-house solution
Other: ……………………………………………………………………

12. Which of the following criteria was the most important when selecting your process management tool? (Make a ranking) Please number each box in order of preference from 1 to 5

☐ Functionality (modelling, simulation capabilities, support of standards, report generation, etc.)

☐ Pricing (Cost of Product)

☐ Support

☐ Positive image and experience of the vendor

☐ Availability of the tool (already used in the company)

12A. Are there any other criteria besides the ones you have ranked in the previous questions?
Please write your answer(s) here:
……………………………………………………………………

SECTION III - PROCESS CHARACTERISTICS

13. List at least one "title" or short description of typical processes in your company/department:
Please write your answer(s) here:
……………………………………………………………………

14. Would you agree to provide us with a description or a model of at least one of these processes as a sample? (under confidentiality agreement) Please choose only one of the following:

☐ Yes
☐ No

* Please choose all that apply

15. To what are your processes related? *

☐ A product of our company
☐ Customer contact
☐ Administration
☐ Systems integration, data transformation
☐ Systems development
☐ Emergency procedure
Other: ………………………………………………………………

16. How did you proceed in describing your processes? *

☐ We started from the products of our company and concentrated on their transformation from an initial to a final form
☐ We started from some goal and grouped the activities to achieve it
☐ We started from the interactions (including data flow) between departments or responsible persons
Other: ………………………………………………………………

17. What triggers the execution of your processes or their tasks? ♦
Please choose the appropriate response for each item:

	All processes	Most processes	Some processes	A few processes	No processes
Information sent from business partners (Customers, suppliers etc.)	☐	☐	☐	☐	☐
Company-internal information	☐	☐	☐	☐	☐
Timing (Date, cycles)	☐	☐	☐	☐	☐
Signals from machines or sensors	☐	☐	☐	☐	☐
Deviations from targets or failures	☐	☐	☐	☐	☐
The state of some process or task	☐	☐	☐	☐	☐
Human judgement and intervention	☐	☐	☐	☐	☐

♦ **Task:** Work that has to be done to achieve some goal in a process; individual steps in processes. Synonym: *Activity*

17A. Are there other things that trigger the execution of your processes or their tasks?
Please write your answer here:
………………………………………………………………

18. What kind of application software is involved in the execution of your processes: *

☐ No software
☐ Business process management system(s)
☐ Enterprise Resource Planning System(s)
☐ Customer Relationship-Management System(s)
☐ Procurement System(s)
☐ System(s) for Production Planning or Supply Chain Management
☐ Product Data Management System
☐ Database(s), Data Warehouse(s)
☐ Content Management System(s)
☐ Production Data Acquisition
☐ Office Software (e.g. text processing, spreadsheet)
☐ Educational software
☐ Application software at business partners
☐ Integration Software, Middleware
Other: ………………………………………………………………

* Please choose all that apply

SECTION IV - PROCESS MODELLING

19. Which entities do you need to describe the processes in your company/department?
Please choose the appropriate response for each item:

	Essential	Frequently needed	Occasionally needed	Rarely needed	Not at all needed
The tasks that have to be done in the process	☐	☐	☐	☐	☐
The relationship between the tasks	☐	☐	☐	☐	☐
The persons or roles who execute the tasks	☐	☐	☐	☐	☐
Resources needed to fulfil the task (e.g. machines, material, documents, software systems, etc.)	☐	☐	☐	☐	☐
Time information related to the task (e.g. durations, start/end time points)	☐	☐	☐	☐	☐
Timely distances between the end of a task and the start of the following task	☐	☐	☐	☐	☐
Events that happen and influence task♦ processing	☐	☐	☐	☐	☐
Documents or objects resulting from a task	☐	☐	☐	☐	☐

♦ **Events**: Pre-modelled incidents that happen within the context of our system or organization

19A. Do you need other entities to describe the processes in your company?
Please write your answer here:
....

20. How often do the following observations apply to the tasks in your processes?
Please choose the appropriate response for each item:

	Always	Very often	Sometimes	Rarely	Never
The tasks follow each other in a strict sequence. In other words, each task has at the most one predecessor and one successor	☐	☐	☐	☐	☐
A task has more than one immediate successor (process splits)	☐	☐	☐	☐	☐
A task has more than one immediate predecessor (process merge)	☐	☐	☐	☐	☐
Some condition (other than the end of the preceding task) must be satisfied in order to start a task	☐	☐	☐	☐	☐
A task (or a group of tasks) is repeated, till some criterion is satisfied	☐	☐	☐	☐	☐
Tasks are alternatives to each other	☐	☐	☐	☐	☐

21. If more than one task can be started, they are performed:
Please choose the appropriate response for each item:

	Always	Very often	Sometimes	Rarely	Never
All and concurrently	☐	☐	☐	☐	☐
All, independent of each other and in any order	☐	☐	☐	☐	☐
Not all tasks are executed	☐	☐	☐	☐	☐
Which task(s) is/are chosen for execution, depends on: - a random selection	☐	☐	☐	☐	☐
- whether or not some condition is satisfied	☐	☐	☐	☐	☐
- the subjective experience of some person in charge	☐	☐	☐	☐	☐
As soon as one task has been executed, no other tasks from the ones that can be started is performed	☐	☐	☐	☐	☐

21A. If the start or the selection of a task depends on a condition, the condition refers to: *

☐ The task only, e.g., the availability of resources
☐ The results of adjacent tasks
☐ The overall state of the process
☐ Information external to the process
☐ Time
Other: ....

22. Which resources do you (wish to) include in the models or descriptions of your processes?
Please choose the appropriate response for each item:

	Essential	Frequently needed	Occasionally needed	Rarely needed	Not at all needed
Machines, appliances	☐	☐	☐	☐	☐
Personnel	☐	☐	☐	☐	☐
Material	☐	☐	☐	☐	☐
Documents	☐	☐	☐	☐	☐
Information	☐	☐	☐	☐	☐
Software Systems	☐	☐	☐	☐	☐

23. Which information about the persons executing a task do you (wish to) include in the models or descriptions of your processes? *

☐ None
☐ The required capabilities (roles, positions)
☐ Names of responsible persons
☐ Organizational units they belong to
Other: ....

[Only answer the question if you answered 'Rarely needed', 'Occasionally needed' or 'Essential' to question Q22]
23A. Which information about the persons executing a task do you (wish to) include in the models or descriptions of your processes? Please write your answer here:
....

24. What kind of additional information do you want to gather in your models?
Please choose the appropriate response for each item:

	Needed for the task	Not needed for the task	Needed for the process	Not needed for the process
Priorities	☐	☐	☐	☐
Cost	☐	☐	☐	☐
Goals	☐	☐	☐	☐
Execution status (e.g., cancelled…)	☐	☐	☐	☐
Planning status (e.g., plan/actual; strategic/tactic)	☐	☐	☐	☐

25. Could you give us at least one example of goals (of processes or tasks) you wish to express?
Please write your answer(s) here:
....

26. Is there any other additional information you want to gather in your models?
Please write your answer here:
....

SECTION V - PROCESS CHANGE

27. How often do you have to change an average process? Please choose **only one** of the following:

☐ In each execution ☐ Daily ☐ Weekly ☐ Monthly ☐ Quarterly ☐ Yearly ☐ Rarely

28. Please assess the amount of change of an average process: *

☐ Minor change ☐ Major change ☐ It depends

* Please choose all that apply

29. Does process change affect only the current execution of the process or all future executions? (i.e. the process description in general): Please choose **only one** of the following:

☐ Only current execution
☐ All future executions
☐ It depends

30. Why do you have to change the processes in your company? *

☐ Because of internal disruptions (e.g. unavailability of resources)
☐ Because of deviations from planned values (e.g. times, cost)
☐ Process change is forced by the environment (e.g. change of laws)
☐ The process evolves in line with the evolving business
☐ The next task to be executed is always determined ad hoc
Other: ....

31. How do you cope with process change or dynamically evolving processes?
Please choose **only one** of the following:

☐ We have predefined process variants
☐ We postpone the selection of tasks or sub-processes to execution time
☐ We apply some change mechanisms
☐ None of the above, specify how you deal with change:
Make a comment on your choice here: ....

[Only answer this question if you answered to Q31]
32. Which change mechanisms do you apply? *

☐ Inserting tasks or subprocesses
☐ Deleting/Skipping tasks or subprocesses
☐ Replacing tasks or subprocesses
☐ Changing the order of tasks or subprocesses
☐ Parallelizing tasks or subprocesses
☐ Serializing tasks or subprocesses
☐ None of the above

SECTION VI - QUANTITATIVE INFORMATION ABOUT YOUR PROCESSES

33. Please assess the following statements about the distribution of the processes in your company:
Please choose the appropriate response for each item:

	All processes	Most processes	Some processes	A few processes	No processes
The processes are executed within the company by one person	☐	☐	☐	☐	☐
The processes are executed within one department, but involve more than one responsible person	☐	☐	☐	☐	☐
The processes are executed within the company by more than one department	☐	☐	☐	☐	☐
The execution of the processes involves also other companies	☐	☐	☐	☐	☐

34. Please estimate the following numbers for an average process in your company (wherever it applies): *

☐ The number of persons from the same department involved in the execution of an average process: ....

☐ The number of departments involved in the execution of an average process: ....

☐ The number of other companies involved in the execution of one of your business processes: ....

☐ The number of application systems involved in the execution of an average process: ....

☐ The number of tasks or activities of an average process: ....

* Please choose all that apply

35. How do you measure the average run time of the processes in your company?
Please choose the appropriate response for each item:

	All processes	Most processes	Some processes	A few processes	No processes
In days	☐	☐	☐	☐	☐
In weeks	☐	☐	☐	☐	☐
In months	☐	☐	☐	☐	☐
In years	☐	☐	☐	☐	☐

36. How often do your execute the processes in your company?
Please choose the appropriate response for each item:

	All processes	Most processes	Some processes	A few processes	No processes
Several times a day	☐	☐	☐	☐	☐
Several times a week	☐	☐	☐	☐	☐
Several times a month	☐	☐	☐	☐	☐
Several times a year	☐	☐	☐	☐	☐

37. If you have any comment, remark, feedback and/or question regarding this questionnaire:
Please write your answer here: …………………………………………..

38. In which country are you located?
Please write your answer here: …………………………………………..

39. To which branch does your company belong to? *
☐ Banking
☐ Conglomerates
☐ Oil & Gas Operations
☐ Consumer Durables
☐ Insurance
☐ Diversified Financials
☐ Telecommunications Service
☐ Retailing
☐ Utilities
☐ Household & Personal Products
☐ Materials
☐ Software & Service
☐ Food, Drink & Tobacco
☐ Technology Hardware & Equipment
☐ Drugs & Biotechnology
☐ Semiconductors
☐ Chemicals
☐ Transportation
☐ Trading Companies
☐ Health Care Equipment & Services
☐ Food Markets
☐ Aerospace & Defence
☐ Media
☐ Construction
☐ Capital Goods
☐ Hotels, Restaurants & Leisure
☐ Business Services & Supplies
Other: ………………………………………………………………………..

40. What is the name of your company?
Please write your answer here: …………………………………………..

41. Please provide us with your name and last name:
Please write your answer here: …………………………………………..

42. Please provide us with your e-mail address (yourname@yourdomain.xy):
Please write your answer here: …………………………………………..

* Please choose all that apply

APPENDIX B:
COVER LETTERS FOR THE QUESTIONNAIRE

u^b

UNIVERSITÄT
BERN

**Institut für
Wirtschaftsinformatik**

Bern, 17th of June 2009

**Empirical Investigation:
Best Practices and Requirements in Process Modelling & Management**

Dear Sir or Madam,

The Department of Information Engineering of the University of Bern (Switzerland), led by Professor Dr.-Ing. Susanne Patig, is currently conducting an empirical investigation about best practices and requirements in process modelling and management. The investigation prepares the ground for a general improvement of process modelling languages and tools. For that reason we want to find out how processes (business processes, software-related or other processes) look like in reality, whether or not they are modelled and if yes, why? Other relevant questions are which constructs are needed in modelling processes, which process-related tools are currently used in companies and which of their functionality is appreciated.

Because of your excellent reputation, your company was selected to participate in this study and your opinion is very important to us. We assure you that your data will be kept confidential. For taking the time in completing this survey, you will have access to the results of this study free of charge and your experiences, requirements and suggestions will be considered in revising existing process modelling languages and tools.

The following link leads you directly to our questionnaire:

http://www2.ie.iwi.unibe.ch/limesurvey/index.php?sid=39112&lang=en

Please forward this link to a person who deals with process modelling and management. Typically, such persons can be found in IT departments, business process management departments, in functional areas (e.g., sales, purchasing) or in product divisions.

We are interested in any type of business or IT process. So, if you know two other process experts in distinct departments, you can send one of the following links to each of them:

Link for Person 2: http://www2.ie.iwi.unibe.ch/limesurvey/index.php?sid=81185&lang=en

Link for Person 3: http://www2.ie.iwi.unibe.ch/limesurvey/index.php?sid=66739&lang=en

Should you have any question or require additional information, don't hesitate to contact me (phone: +41 31 631 49 67, e-mail: Susanne.patig@iwi.unibe.ch) or my assistant, Mrs. Vanessa Casanova-Brito (phone: +41 31 631 33 74, e-mail: Vanessa.Casanova-Brito@iwi.unibe.ch).

In order to continue with our study in a timely manner, we would appreciate to get your answers until the end of next week.

Thank you very much for your participation.

Kind regards

Susanne Patig

Prof. Dr.-Ing. habil. Susanne Patig
Engehaldenstrasse 8
CH-3012 Bern

+41 (0)31 631 49 67
+41 (0)31 631 46 82
susanne.patig@iwi.unibe.ch
http://www.ap.iwi.unibe.ch/

u^b

b
UNIVERSITÄT
BERN

Institut für
Wirtschaftsinformatik

Bern, 2009-06-17

Empirische Untersuchung:
Best Practices und Anforderungen in der Prozessmodellierung

Sehr geehrte Damen und Herren,

gegenwärtig führt die Universität Bern, Abteilung Information Engineering (Prof. Dr.-Ing. habil. Susanne Patig), eine empirische Untersuchung zu Best Practices und Anforderungen in der Prozessmodellierung durch. Ziel der Untersuchung ist es, die praktische Anwendbarkeit der vorhandenen Modellierungssprachen und Softwarewerkzeuge zu verbessern. Deshalb wollen wir wissen, wie Prozesse in der Realität aussehen, ob und wie sie modelliert werden und wofür die Modelle genutzt werden. Typische Fragen betreffen z. B. die für die Modellierung benötigten Konstrukte, die Größe der Prozessmodelle, die verwendeten Softwarewerkzeuge und die durch Prozesse zu integrierenden Informationssysteme. Prozesse im Sinne der Untersuchung sind sowohl Geschäftsprozesse als auch IT-Prozesse (z.B. Softwareentwicklungsprozesse, Nachrichten- und Kontrollflüsse in Integrationsszenarien etc.).

Ihr Unternehmen wurde aufgrund seiner herausragenden Reputation als eines der zu befragenden ausgewählt, Ihre Antworten sind von großer Bedeutung für uns. Wir versichern Ihnen, dass Ihre Daten vertraulich behandelt werden. Im Gegenzug erhalten Sie kostenfrei die vollständige Ergebnisdokumentation der Befragung. Außerdem werden Ihre Erfahrungen, Anforderungen und Vorschläge bei der Überarbeitung der bestehenden Prozessmodellierungssprachen und Werkzeuge berücksichtigt.

Der folgende Link führt Sie direkt zu unseren Fragebogen:

http://www2.ie.iwi.unibe.ch/limesurvey/index.php?sid=39112&lang=en

Bitte leiten Sie diesen Link weiter an eine Person, die mit Prozessmodellierung und -management befasst ist. Typischerweise finden sich solche Personen in IT-Abteilungen, Business-Process- Management-Teams, in Funktionsbereichen (z. B. Vertrieb, Einkauf) oder in Produktsparten.

Wir interessieren uns für alle Arten von Geschäfts- oder IT-Prozessen. Wenn Sie weitere Prozess-Experten in anderen Abteilungen kennen, dann schicken Sie bitte je einen der folgenden Links an diese Personen:

Link für Person 2: http://www2.ie.iwi.unibe.ch/limesurvey/index.php?sid=81185&lang=en

Link für Person 3: http://www2.ie.iwi.unibe.ch/limesurvey/index.php?sid=66739&lang=en

Sollten Sie Fragen haben oder zusätzliche Informationen benötigen, können Sie sich gern an mich wenden (Tel.: +41 31 631 49 67, E-Mail: Susanne.Patig@iwi.unibe.ch) oder an meine Assistentin, Frau Casanova-Brito (Tel.: +41 31 631 33 74, E-Mail: Vanessa.Casanova-Brito@iwi.unibe.ch).

Um rasch mit unserer Untersuchung fortfahren zu können, würden wir uns freuen, Ihre Antwort bis zum Ende der nächsten Woche zu erhalten.

Vielen Dank für Ihre Kooperation.

Freundliche Grüsse

Susanne Patig

Prof. Dr.-Ing. habil. Susanne Patig
Engehaldenstrasse 8
CH-3012 Bern

+41 (0)31 631 49 67
+41 (0)31 631 46 82
susanne.patig@iwi.unibe.ch
http://www.ap.iwi.unibe.ch/

Berna, 1ro. de Junio 2009

**Institut für
Wirtschaftsinformatik**

Investigacion Empirica:
Mejores Practicas y Requerimientos en Manejo y Modelos de Procesos

Estimados Señores y Señoras:

El Departamento de Sistemas de Informacion de la Universidad de Berna (Suiza), a cargo de la Dra. Ing. Susanne Patig, esta actualmente realizando una investigacion academica sobre mejores practicas y requerimientos de modelos y manejo de procesos. Esta investigacion preparara el terreno para una mejora general de los lenguajes y herramientas existentes para modelar los procesos. Por esa razon nuestro objetivo es investigar como los procesos (procesos corporativos, procesos relacionados con softwares u otros procesos) se ven en realidad, si los procesos estan siendo modelados actualmente y porque?. Otras preguntas de gran importancia son entre otras, los constructos que son necesarios para modelar los procesos, que herramientas de procesos estan siendo utilizados en la compañia y que funciones son apreciadas.

Por su excelente reputacion, su compañia ha sido seleccionada para participar en nuestra investigacion. Su opinion es muy importante para nosotros. Le aseguramos que mantendremos la informacion de manera confidencial. Por tomarse el tiempo en completar nuestro cuestionario, Ud. tendra accesso a los resultados de este studio sin ningun costo alguno. De la misma manera, sus experiencias, requerimientos y sugerencias seran consideradas en las futuras revisiones de dichos lenguajes y herramientas de procesos existentes hoy en dia.

El siguiente enlace lo llevara directamente a nuestro cuestionario:

http://www2.ie.iwi.unibe.ch/limesurvey/index.php?sid=39112&lang=en

Le rogamos enviar este enlace a la persona encargada de modelar y manejar los procesos en su compañia. Generalmente ellos se encuentran en el departamento de IT, (o en su defecto al CIO, Chief Information Officer), en el departamento de business process management o en alguna area funcional (departamento de ventas o compras) o en divisiones de productos.

Estamos interesado en cualquier tipo de procesos IT o procesos corporativos. Si Ud. conociera otros dos expertos en procesos en otros departamentos, por favor enviele uno de los siguientes enlaces a cada uno de ellos:

Enlace para persona 1:
http://www2.ie.iwi.unibe.ch/limesurvey/index.php?sid=81185&lang=en

Enlace para persona 2:
http://www2.ie.iwi.unibe.ch/limesurvey/index.php?sid=66739&lang=en

No dude en contactarse conmigo si tuviera alguna pregunta o requiera mas informacion. (Telefono: +41 31 631 49 67, e-mail: Susanne.patig@iwi.unibe.ch) o con mi asistenta la Sra. Vanessa Casanova-Brito (Telefono: +41 31 631 33 74, e-mail: Vanessa.Casanova-Brito@iwi.unibe.ch).

Para continuar con nuestra investigacion de manera rapida, le rogamos nos envie una respuesta hasta finales de la proxima semana.

Muy agradecida por su participacion.

Cordiales saludos

Susanne Patig

Prof. Dr.–Ing. habil. Susanne Patig +41 (0)31 631 49 67
Engehaldenstrasse 8 +41 (0)31 631 46 82
CH-3012 Bern susanne.patig@iwi.unibe.ch
 http://www.ap.iwi.unibe.ch/

u^b

UNIVERSITÄT
BERN

Institut für
Wirtschaftsinformatik

Bern, 25th of June 2009

**Empirical Investigation:
Best Practices and Requirements in Process Modelling & Management**

拝啓

-ing博士率いる、ベルン大学（スイス）情報工学部において、Susanne Patigは現在、プロセスモデリング・マネージメントにおける、最良の実習と資格についての実質調査をしております。この調査は、プロセスモデリング言語・ツールの一般的な改良への基礎基盤となります。この理由から、私達はビジネスプロセス、ソフトウェアプロセスなどのプロセスが、実際にどのように機能しているのかを知りたいのです。そしてまた、以下の質問があります。どの構成概念がモデリングプロセスにおいて必要とされ、そのプロセスリレーティッドツールが現在、会社において使用され、また、どの機能が評価されているのでしょうか？

貴社はこの研究対象として選考され、貴方の意見はとても重要なものになるでしょう。私達は、貴方の調査データを機密情報として扱う事を確約いたします。この調査において、貴方はこの研究の結果を無償で閲覧する事ができ、また貴方の経験、資格、そして提案などは既存のプロセスモデリング言語・ツールを修正する際に尊重されるでしょう。

以下のリンクは、直接私達の調査結果と繋がっています。http://www2.ie.iwi.unibe.ch/limesurvey/index.php?sid=39112&lang=en
このリンクを、プロセスモデリング・マネージメントを扱う担当の方へ転送願います。一般的に、そういった担当の方々は、ＩＴ部門や、ビジネスプロセス・マネージメント部門などにいらっしゃるかと思います。

We are interested in any type of business or IT process. So, if you know two other process experts in distinct departments, you can send one of the following links to each of them:
Link for Person 2:
http://www2.ie.iwi.unibe.ch/limesurvey/index.php?sid=81185&lang=en
Link for Person 3:
http://www2.ie.iwi.unibe.ch/limesurvey/index.php?sid=66739&lang=en

Should you have any question or require additional information, don't hesitate to contact me (phone: +41 31 631 49 67, e-mail: Susanne.patig@iwi.unibe.ch) or my assistant Mrs. Vanessa Casanova-Brito (phone: +41 31 631 33 74, e-mail: Vanessa.Casanova-Brito@iwi.unibe.ch).

私達の研究を迅速に継続するため、返答を翌週末までに頂けるようお願い致します。

御協力ありがとうございます。
敬具
Susanne Patig

Prof. Dr.–Ing. habil. Susanne Patig   +41 (0)31 631 49 67
Engehaldenstrasse 8   +41 (0)31 631 46 82
CH-3012 Bern   susanne.patig@iwi.unibe.ch
http://www.ap.iwi.unibe.ch/

REFERENCES

[BeKP09]
Becker, J., Knackstedt, R., Pöppelbuss, J.: Developing maturity models for IT management – A procedure model and its application. Business & Information Systems Engineering 3, pp. 213-222. (2009)

[BeKR03]
Becker, J., Kugeler, M., Rosemann, M.: Process Management – A Guide for the Design of Business Processes. Springer, Berlin et al. (2003)

[BiLN00]
Bilder, C. R., Loughin, T. M., Nettleton, D.: Multiple marginal independence testing for pick any/c variables. Communications in Statistics: Simulation 29, pp. 1285-1316. (2000)

[Chan06]
Chang, J. F.: Business process management systems – Strategy and implementation. Auerbach Publications. (2006)

[CMM06]
CMMI Product Team: Capability Maturity Model Integration (CMMI) for Development, Version 1.2. Document Number: CMU/SEI-2006-TR-008 ESC-TR. Carnegie Mellon Software Engineering Institute, Pittsburgh, PA 15213-3890. (2006)

[CuAl06]
Curtis, B., Alden, J.: BPM & Organizational Maturity, BPTrends Reports, November 2006. (2006)

[EIU08]
Economist Intelligence Unit (in cooperation with the IBM Institute for Business Value): E-readiness rankings 2008: Maintaining momentum. A white paper from the Economist Intelligence Unit. London et al. http://www.eiu.com/site_info.asp?info_name=ibm_ereadiness&page=noads&rf=0. (2008)

[Fisc04]
Fischer, D. M.: The Business Process Maturity Model – A Practical Approach for Identifying Opportunities for Optimization. BP Trends Reports. September 2004. (2004)

[Forb00]
Forbes: The Forbes Global 2000. http://www.forbes.com/lists/2008/18/biz_2000global08_The-Global-2000_Rank.html. (2000)

[GrRo00]
Green, P., Rosemann, M.: Integrated process modeling: An ontological evaluation Information Systems. In Proceedings of the 11th International Conference of Advanced Information Systems Engineering. (Stockholm, Sweden, June 05-09, 2000). CAiSE 2000. Elsevier, vol. 25, No. 2, pp. 73-87. DOI= http://dx.doi.org/10.1016/S0306-4379(00)00010-7. (2000)

[GrWa09]
Gravetter, F. J., Wallnau, L. B.: Statistics for the Behavioral Sciences. 8th ed., Wadsworth, Belmont. (2009)

[Harm04]
Harmon, P.: Evaluating an Organization's Business Process Maturity, BPTrends Reports, March 2004. (2004)

[Holt09]
Holt, J.: A Pragmatic Guide to Business Process Modeling. 2nd ed., BCS, Swindon. (2009)

[InRR09a]
Indulska, M., Recker, J., Rosemann, M., Green, P.: Business Process Modeling: Perceived Benefits. In Proceedings of the 28th International Conference on Conceptual Modeling (Gramado, Brazil, November 09-12, 2009). ER 2009. LNCS, Vol. 5829, pp. 458-471. Springer, Berlin. (2009)

[InRR09b]
Indulska, M., Recker, J., Rosemann, M., Green, P.: Business Process Modeling: Current issues and future challenges. In: van Eck, P. et al. (eds.): Proceedings of the 21st International Conference of Advanced Information Systems Engineering (Amsterdam, The Netherlands, June 8-12, 2009). CAiSE 2009. LNCS, vol. 5565, pp. 501-514. Springer, Berlin (2009)

[JaBS06]
Jaklic, J., Bosilj-Vuksic, V., Stemberger, M.I.: Business Process Oriented Tool Selection Model – A Case Study. In: Hlupic, V. et al. (eds.) 1st International Conference on Future Challenges and Current Issues in Business Information. Organization and Process Management 2006, pp. 94-102. Westminster Business School, London (2006)

[Jack09]
Jackson, S.L.: Research Methods and Statistics: A Critical Thinking Approach. 3rd ed., Wadsworth, Belmont (2009)

[Krus52]
Kruskal, W. H.: A nonparametric test for the several sample problem. The Annals of Mathematical Statistics, 23(4), pp. 525-540. (1952)

[KüHa07]
Küng, P., Hagen, C.: The fruits of Business Process Management: an experience report from a Swiss bank. Business Process Management Journal 13, pp. 477-487 (2007)

[LeLK07]
Lee, J., Lee, D., Kang, S.: An overview of the business process maturity model. In: Chang, K. C. et al. (eds.): Proceedings of the joint 9th Asia-Pacific Web Conference, APWeb 2007, and 8th International Conference, on Web-Age Information

Management, WAIM 2007 (Huang Shan, China, June 16-18, 2007). APWeb/WAIM 2007 Ws. LNCS, vol. 4537, pp. 84-395. Springer, Berlin. (2007)

[LiKo06]
List, B., Korherr, B.: An evaluation of conceptual business process modelling languages. In: Proceedings of the Association for Computing Machinery Symposium on Applied Computing (Dijon, France, April 23-27, 2006). ACM, New York, NY, pp. 1532-1539. DOI= http://doi.acm.org/10.1145/1141277.1141633. (2006)

[Lime09]
Limesurvey, Version 1.85, http://www.limesurvey.org/

[LiYP02]
Lin, F., Yang, M., Pai, Y.: A Generic Structure for Business Process Modeling. Business Process Management Journal 8, 1, pp. 19-41. (2002)

[McJo01]
Mccormack, K. P., Johnsohn, W. C.: Business Process Orientation – Gaining the E-Business Competitive Advantage. St. Lucie Press, Boca Raton et al. (2001)

[McWB+09]
McCormack, K. et al.: A global investigation of key turning points in business process maturity. Business Process Management Journal 15, pp. 792-815 (2009)

[MeRC07]
Mendling, J., Reijers, H.A., Cardoso, J.: What Makes Process Models Understandable? In: Proceedings of the 5th International Conference on Business Process Management (Brisbane, Australia, September 24-29, 2007). BPM 2007. LNCS, vol. 4717, pp. 48-63. Springer, Berlin. (2007)

[MeSi06]
Melenovsky, M., Sinur, J.: BPM Maturity Model Identifies Six Phases for Successful BPM Adoption. Gartner Research. ID Number: G00142643. Publication Date: 18 October 2006. (2006)

[Neub09]
Neubauer, T.: An empirical study about the status of business process management. Business Process Management Journal 15, pp. 166-183. (2009)

[NIST93]
NIST- National Institute Of Standards and Technology: Integration Definition for function modeling (IDEF0). http://www.idef.com/pdf/idef0.pdf. (1993)

[NoBJ10]
Norton, D., Blechar, M., Jones, T.: Magic Quadrant for Business Process Analysis Tools. Gartner RAS Core Research Note G00174515, 22 February 2010. (2010)

[OASIS07]
Organization for the Advancement of Structured Information Standards (OASIS): Web Services Business Process Execution Language Version 2.0, OASIS Standard ,11 April 2007, http://docs.oasis-open.org/wsbpel/2.0/wsbpel-v2.0.pdf (2007)

[OMG07]
Object Management Group (OMG): OMG Unified Modeling Language (OMG UML), Superstructure, Version 2.1.1. OMG Document Number: formal/2007-02-05. http://www.omg.org/technology/documents/formal/uml.htm. (2007)

[OMG08]
Object Management Group (OMG): Business Process Maturity Model (BPMM). OMG document number: formal/2008-06-01. http://www.omg.org/spec/BPMM/1.0/PDF. (2008)

[OMG09]
Object Management Group (OMG): Business Process Model and Notation (BPMN), Version 1.2. OMG document number: formal/2009-01-0. http://www.omg.org/spec/BPMN/1.2. (2009)

[OMG10]
Object Management Group (OMG): OMG Unified Modeling Language (OMG UML), Superstructure, Version 2.3. OMG document number: dtc/2010-05-05. http://www.omg.org/technology/documents/formal/uml.htm. (2010)

[OMG11]
Object Management Group (OMG): Business Process Model and Notation (BPMN), Version 2.0. OMG document number: formal/2011-01-03. http://www.omg.org/spec/BPMN/2.0/. (2011)

[PaCV10]
Patig, S., Casanova-Brito, V., Vögeli, B.: IT Requirements of Business Process Management in Practice – An Empirical Study. In: Hull, R., Mendling, J., Tai. S. (eds.): Proceedings of the 8th International Conference on Business Process Management. (Hoboken, USA, September 13-16, 2010). BPMN 2010. LNCS 6336, pp.13-28. Springer, Berlin. (2010)

[PaCa11]
Patig, S., Casanova-Brito, V.: Requirements of process modeling languages – Results from an empirical investigation. In: Bernstein, A., Schwabe, G., (eds.): Proceedings 10th International Conference Wirtschaftsinformatik, (Zurich, 16-18 February, 2011). (2011)

[PaCC93]
Paulk, M. C., Curtis, B., Chrissis, M. B., Weber, C. V.: Capability Maturity Model for Software, Version 1.1. Software Engineering Institute, Carnegie Mellon University. Technical Report CMU/SEI-93-TR-024. ESC-TR-93-177. February 1993. (1993)

[Pati04]
    Patig, S.: Measuring Expressiveness in Conceptual Modeling. In: Proceedings of the 16th International Conference of Advanced Information Systems Engineering. (Riga, Latvia, June 07-11, 2004). CAiSE 2004. Springer, Berlin et al. LNCS Vol. 3084, pp. 127-141. (2004)

[PrAr99]
    Pritchard, J.-P., Armisted, C.: Business process management – Lessons from European Business. Business Process Management Journal 5, pp. 10-35 (1999)

[Reck08]
    Recker, J.: BPMN Modeling – Who, where, how and why. BPTrends, March 2008. http://www.sparxsystems.com/press/articles/pdf/bpmn_survey.pdf. (2008)

[ReDr07]
    Recker, J., Dreiling, A.: Does It Matter Which Process Modeling Language We Teach or Use? An Experimental Study on Understanding Process Modelling Languages without Formal Education. In: Proceedings of the 18th Australasian Conference on Information Systems (Toowoomba, Australia, December 05-07, 2007). ACIS 2007. (2007)

[ReIR+06]
    Recker, J., Indulska, M., Rosemann, M., Green, P.: How Good is BPMN Really? Insights from Theory and Practice. In: Proceedings of the 14th European Conference on Information Systems (Göteborg, Sweden, June 12–14, 2006). ECIS 2006. (2006)

[ReMS+09]
    Recker, J., zur Muehlen, M., Siau, K., Erickscon, J., Indulska, M.: Measuring Method Complexity: UML versus BPMN. In: Proceedings of the 15th Americas Conference on Information Systems (San Francisco, California, August 06–09, 2009). AMCIS 2009. AISeL, Paper 541. http://aisel.aisnet.org/amcis2009/541. (2009)

[ReRK07]
    Recker, J., Rosemann, M., Krogstie, J.: Ontology- Versus Pattern-Based Evaluation of Process Modeling Languages: A Comparison. In Communications of the Association for Information Systems. 20, Article 48 (2007). http://aisel.aisnet.org/cais/vol20/iss1/48. (2007)

[RoBr05]
    Rosemann, M., de Bruin, T.: Application of a holistic model for determining BPM maturity. BPTrends Reports, February 2005. (2005)

[RoBr06]
    Rosemann, M., de Bruin, T., Power, B.: BPM maturity. In: Jeston, J., Nelis, J. (eds.): Business Process Management: Practical Guidelines to Successful Implementations. 2nd edition. Butterwoth-Heinemann, Amsterdam et al. (2006)

[RoBH04]
    Rosemann, M., de Bruin, T., Hueffner, T.: A Model for Business Process Management Maturity. In: Proceedings of the 15th Australasian Conference on Information Systems. ACIS 2004, Paper 6. http://aisel.aisnet.org/acis2004/6. (2004)

[Rohl09]
    Rohloff, M.: Case study and maturity model for business process management implementation. In: Dayal, U. et al., (eds.): Proceedings of the 7th Conference on Business Process Management. BPM 2009. LNCS 5701, pp. 128-142. Springer, Berlin (2009)

[RuHA+06]
    Russell, N., ter Hofstede, A.H.M., van der Aalst, W., Mulyar, N.: Workflow control-flow patterns – A revised view. BPM Center Report BPM-06-22, BPMcenter.org. 2006. http://www.workflowpatterns.com/documentation/documents/BPM-06-22.pdf. (2006)

[Schm08]
    Schmietendorf, A.: Assessment of Business Process Modeling Tools under Consideration of Business Process Management Activities. In: Dumke, R. et al. (Eds.): Proceedings of Software Process and Product Measurement, International Conferences Metrikon / Mensura 2008. IWSM 2008. LNCS 5338, pp. 141–154. Springer, Berlin. (2008)

[ScTA05]
    Scheer, A.-W., Thomas, O., Adam, T.: Process Modeling Using Event-driven Process Chains. In: Dumas, M., van der Aalst, W., ter Hofstede, A.H.M. (eds.): Process-Aware Information Systems. Wiley, Hoboken, New Jersey, pp. 119-145. (2005)

[Seid10]
    Seidlmeier, H.: Prozessoptimierung mit dem ARIS Toolset. 3n ed., Vieweg, Wiesbaden (2010) (in German)

[SiHi10]
    Sinur, J., Hill, J.B.: Magic Quadrant for Business Process Management Suites. Gartner RAS Core Research Note G00205212, 18 October 2010. (2010)

[SmMM09]
    Smart, P. A., Maddern, H., Maull, R. S.: Understanding business process management – Implications for theory and practice. British Journal of Management 20, pp. 491-507. (2009)

[SöAJ+02]
Söderström, E., Andersson, B., Johannesson, P., Perjons, E., Wangler, B.: Towards a Framework for Comparing Process Modeling Languages. In Proceedings of the 14th International Conference of Advanced Information Systems Engineering. (Toronto, Canada, May 27 - 31, 2002). CAiSE 2002. LNCS, vol. 2348, pp. 600-611. Springer, Berlin. (2002)

[SPSS10]
SPSS: SPSS Statistics, Version 17.0. http.//www.spss.com (2010)

[vAvH04]
van der Aalst, W., van Hee, K.: Workflow Management: Models, Methods and Systems. MIT Press, Cambridge. (2004)

[vAtH10]
van der Aalst, W., ter Hofstede, A.: Workflow Patterns Home Page. http://www.workflowpatterns.com/patterns/index.php. (2010)

[Webe97]
Weber, R.: Ontological foundations of information systems. Coopers & Lybrand, Blackburn (1997)

[Wesk07]
Weske, M.: Business Process Management: Concepts, Languages, Architectures. Springer, Berlin (2007)

[WfMC95]
The Workflow Management Coalition (WfMC): The Workflow Reference Model. Document Number TC00-1003, Issue 1.1., 19 November 1995, http://www.wfmc.org/standards/ docs/tc003v11.pdf. (1995)

[WfMC99]
The Workflow Management Coalition (WfMC). Terminology & Glossary. Document Number WFMC-TC-1011, Issue 3.0, February 1999. http://www.wfmc.org/standards/docs/TC-1011_term_glossary_v3.pdf. (1999)

[WfMC08]
The Workflow Management Coalition (WfMC). Process Definition Interface - XML Process Definition Language (XPDL). Document Number WFMC-TC-1025, 10 October 2008, Version 2.1a. http://www.wfmc.org/xpdl.html. (2008)

[WoHa10]
Wolf, C., Harmon, P.: The State of Business Process Management 2010. BPTrends Reports, February 2010, http://www.bptrends.com/surveys_landing.cfm. (2010)

[zuMu04]
zur Muehlen, M.: Workflow-based process controlling: Foundation, design and application of workflow-driven process information systems. Logos, Berlin. (2004)

[zMRI07]
zur Muehlen, M., Recker, J., Indulska, M.: Sometimes less is more: Are process modeling languages overly complex? In: Proceedings of the 11th International IEEE EDOC Conference Workshop (Annapolis, MD, USA, October 15-16, 2007). EDOC '07. pp. 197-204. (2007)

[zMRI08]
zur Muehlen, M., Recker, J., Indulska, M.. How Much Language is Enough? Theoretical and Practical Use of the Business Process Modeling Notation. In: Bellahsêne, Z., Léonard, M. (eds.): Proceedings of the 20th International Conference of Advanced Information Systems Engineering. (Montpellier, France, June 16-17, 2008). CAiSE 2008. LNCS, vol. 5074, pp. 465-479. Springer, Berlin. DOI= http://dx.doi.org/10.1007/978-3-540-69534-9_35. (2008)

We would like to thank Dr. Karin Timme of the Frank & Timme publishing company for her flexibility and patience in finding the right layout for giant data records, and Louise Gough, Northamptonshire, for proofreading the final manuscript.